A WALKER'S GUIDE TO THE
LANCASTER CANAL

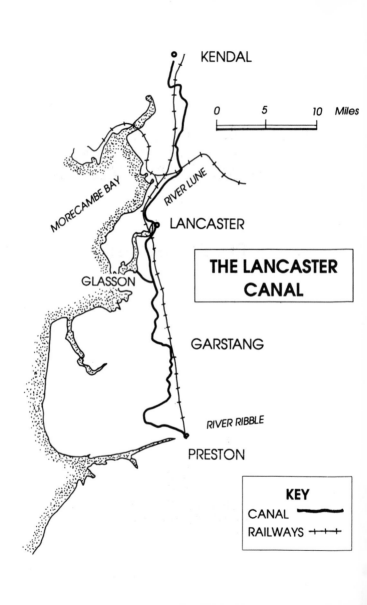

KENDAL

0   5   10   Miles

MORECAMBE BAY

RIVER LUNE

LANCASTER

THE LANCASTER
CANAL

GLASSON

GARSTANG

RIVER RIBBLE

PRESTON

KEY
CANAL
RAILWAYS +++

A WALKER'S GUIDE TO THE
LANCASTER CANAL

BY

ROBERT SWAIN

CICERONE PRESS
MILNTHORPE CUMBRIA

Front Cover: Angling near Chorley's Bridge, Bolton-le-Sands
Back Cover: Looking towards Bolton Turnpike Bridge from near
Bolton Church Bridge, Bolton-le-Sands

Contents

* * *

Foreword

Over the years there have been many changes on the Lancaster Canal, as will be seen in this book. During my boyhood there were very few boats passing along, cruising not then being as popular as it is today. No doubt there will be many changes to come, hopefully for the benefit of the canal and all those who derive pleasure from it.

This book does not claim to be a complete history of the canal. There are many gaps in its story as things which were looked upon as commonplace at the time and went unremarked would now be of real historical interest. Therefore all opinions expressed and conclusions drawn are my own; further information could, as always, come to light to prove or disprove them at a later stage.

Part One: The Canal Story

CHAPTER ONE:
CONCEPTION AND CONSTRUCTION

The Lancaster Canal is a child of the canal fever of the 1700's whose promotion came largely from Lancaster itself. In those times Lancaster was a more important town than Preston and a competitor as a port with Liverpool. Communications were bad, so much so that it was actually cheaper to import foreign goods to the town than to bring English goods from places such as Wigan and Manchester! Roads were in a terrible condition; according to an account of 1768 by the topographer Arthur Young, between Preston and Wigan there were ruts 4 feet deep floating with mud. He passed three carts which had broken down. Tongue in cheek he wrote that, in winter "it would have cost no more money to make the roads navigable than to make them hard." Perhaps a bit of an exaggerated claim, but still giving an impression of conditions.

The constantly shifting sands of the tidal Lune made Lancaster a difficult port to enter. The original port, at Sunderland Point on the north side of the estuary, was superseded by the construction of St. George's Quay just below the town. Glasson Dock was finished 5 miles further down the Lune in 1787, complete with a fully equipped wet dock. However the sandbanks of the outer estuary still had to be negotiated, so in 1799 a scheme was promoted to build a new dock at Thornbush which, with the aid of a canal through into Lancaster would replace Glasson Dock. This scheme would have overcome the silting problems but was abandoned because the West India trade declined.

Coal reached Lancaster and the surrounding district by sea from the River Douglas, making it an expensive commodity. The same supply line served the Kendal area through the port of Milnthorpe at the mouth of the River Bela on the Kent estuary. At that time both south Westmorland and north Lancashire had a plentiful supply of limestone to be burnt into the agricultural lime required for use in the arable country further south. This was the background against which the Lancaster Canal was conceived.

Originally it was proposed that a canal be built from a junction with the Leeds-Liverpool Canal at Walton-le-Dale, through Preston and Lancaster to Kendal. In the late 1760's it was further suggested that this line be continued on from Walton to Worsley, near Manchester, where it would join the Bridgewater Canal, England's first modern canal. At a meeting held at Lancaster town hall on November 13th, 1771 which proposed a canal northwards from the Leeds and Liverpool, it was decided that a survey should be made. James Brindley was approached and commenced the survey but had to relinquish the task to his pupil Robert Whitworth owing to ill health. Whitworth put forward a plan in 1772 for a canal from the proposed Leeds and Liverpool near Eccleston, crossing the Ribble below Penwortham Bridge, travelling over the Fylde Plain almost to Kirkham, then back eastwards nearly to Barton and finally north again. The Lune crossing was to be below Skerton Bridge at Lancaster. The long level of 54.5 miles terminated at Tewitfield to the north of Carnforth where there was to be a rise of 86 feet, the remaining 18 miles to Kendal being level again.

This line did not satisfy the committee who asked Whitworth to try to find an easier Lune crossing. He took a higher line, locking up 24 feet from the Ribble at Sidegreave. From there the course was to Salwick Hall, then eastward again to Hough where it turned north to pass to the east of Garstang and Lancaster with a long hair-pin bend nearly to Halton, and from there on to Tewitfield, a grand total of 55.5 miles. He observed that "notwithstanding the 24 feet rise, this was the easier and better line." At Tewitfield a rise of 62 feet was necessary and the line there followed a very similar line to the canal's existing course through Holme, Farleton, Crooklands and Hincaster Tunnel to Kendal. All this was, of course, done without the aid of modern surveying instruments. The committee were still not satisfied; they sought further advice on easier ways to cross the Ribble and the Lune, one

Hollowforth Aqueduct, Lancaster Canal, Preston

of which was by taking a line as far up as Halton Scars. Each surveyor came to the conclusion that it was necessary to drop to Whitworth's line. A major objection to the scheme was that the course did not extend far enough south to reach the Wigan coalfields.

In 1781 there was a survey made for a canal from Ingleton and Burton-in-Lonsdale to join the Lune at or near Lancaster, but it came to nothing.

A further scheme was put forward by John Wilkinson, the ironmaster of Castle Head near Lindale. His scheme, probably originated with John Jenkinson of Yealand, was to enclose and drain 38,710 acres of Morecambe Bay at a cost of £150,000. John Longbotham, who surveyed the scheme, proposed closing the sands and building a channel from the River Winster where it entered the Kent Estuary, across Foulshaw Moss to Nether Levens. Here it would join the River Kent which would be diverted along the coast to Arnside. It would then cut through the isthmus to join the coast again near Warton Crag and follow the coastline to Heysham Head where it would enter the sea.. The channel was to be navigable from the Kent to Bare where a short canal would be cut across to the Lune almost opposite Lancaster. Presumably there was insufficient support for the idea as nothing came of this one either.

1791 saw patience running short. By then it was considered to be a matter of necessity to Kendal, Lancaster and perhaps Preston to get on a footing with their southern neighbours or to submit to a decline in their trade and population. On June 4th, 1791 thirty merchants and traders of Lancaster presented a petition to the mayor asking him to convene a public meeting to consider making a canal linking it with the Leeds and Liverpool. The petition set forth the advantages held by their rival port of Liverpool as a result of having inland navigation:

"The advantages the town of Liverpool has derived from their inland navigations, and so much increased from the progress of the Canal towards Leeds, which is going forward with great spirit. The completion whereof and those projected cutts (*sic*) to Bury, Bolton, etc. which are in agitation with little doubt of success, will add further benefit, and give the merchants and traders in that place so decided a superiority in the vend of their imports as greatly to diminish the commerce of this town, and its consequences, materially affect the landed interest in the neighbourhood, unless some means can be found to meet them in the market upon more equal terms."

The outcome of the resultant public meeting on June 8th was a resolution to promote a canal and a subscription list was opened.

Samuel Gregson of Lancaster was appointed as clerk. Longbotham, Robert Dickinson of Gargrave and Richard Beck were, during the next few months, asked to resurvey Whitworth's line and also extend it southwards to Worsley, but they were unable to find a better alternative.

In October 1791 John Rennie, the engineer, was asked to make a survey, the committee being undecided whether to make for the Manchester, Bolton and Bury Canal or the Bridgewater Canal. Rennie worked fast during the December of that year and January 1792 and came up with a plan for a broad canal which was accepted. The line was to commence at Westhoughton, situated in the coalfield midway between Bolton and Wigan, thus making a canal of twice the value to the districts it would serve. It was to continue on the level for 15.5 miles to Clayton Green, Lock down 222 feet in a flight of thirty-two locks to an embankment across the Ribble Valley, then cross the river by aqueduct to Preston. Beyond this Whitworth's upper line was to be followed as far as the Calder where Rennie desired a branch to go round the north side of Greenalgh Castle to Garstang, cross the Wyre by an aqueduct, then join the line again at Cabus Nook. At Ashton, to the south of Lancaster, there was to be a deep cutting and the Lune would be crossed further downstream. The canal would then travel onwards to Tewitfield, a level 42.5 miles. Here he proposed a flight of five locks, with another four near Milton where he rejoined Whitworth's line, making a total rise of 65 feet. In order that the canal could serve Wakefield's gunpowder mills at Sedgwick it was still necessary to tunnel through Hincaster Hill. A further 5 miles took the canal to Kendal, making a total length of 75.5 miles. In addition Rennie added two branches to the main line, one from Chorley to Duxbury (3 miles) and the other from Tewitfield to Warton Crag (2.5 miles), neither of which was ever constructed in the end.

A general meeting was held in Lancaster town hall on February 7th, 1792 when it was "Resolved unanimously that a subscription should be entered into for obtaining an Act of Parliament to carry the said canal into execution and the defraying all expenses necessary for completing same." £247,800 is said to have been promised before the meeting terminated, a sum which had risen to £370,500 before the end of the month.

By now it was essential that an Act of Parliament was obtained as soon as possible as the Leeds and Liverpool Canal backers were

Looking towards Myerscough Bridge, Bilsborrow

proposing to alter their line to one nearly parallel to the Lancaster
one between Whittle-le-Woods and Wigan. Negotiations took
place between the Lancaster committee and those for the Leeds
and Liverpool, and the Manchester, Bolton and Bury canals.
However, opposition to the Lancaster's Bill failed and it was
passed by Parliament on June 25th, 1792, authorising Rennie's
line and branches and junctions with possible future canals
(which were never constructed) from the Fylde, Hornby, Ingleton
and Kirkby Lonsdale. Water was to be taken from the River Mint
at Mintsfeet, Kendal, provision being made for mill owners to
draw, if necessary, from the canal provided that its level did not
drop to less than 5 feet. The authorised share capital was £414,000
divided into £100 shares. £60,000 was to be set aside solely for the
Westmorland section. Additionally, permission was given to bor-
row an extra £200,000 if needed. Duties on coal were fixed at 2s 3d
per ton (maximum) descending the locks to the Ribble and not

proceeding more than 18 miles north of Chorley, with 1^1/2d per ton/ mile elsewhere.

Amongst the petitioners for the canal were John Dilworth (who was elected chairman of the Lancaster Canal Company at the first meeting of the proprietors on July 3rd, 1792) and Thomas Worswick (elected treasurer), both bankers of Lancaster. John Brockbank, a Lancaster shipbuilder, the Earl of Balcarres, a coal-owner, John Wakefield and Thomas Crewdson of Kendal and further prominent people of the two towns were other petitioners.

The canal committee was formed mainly of Lancaster men, there being only one each from Preston and Kendal. They appointed John Rennie engineer in July 1792 at £600 p.a.. He was required to reside at Lancaster for five months a year and give attendance as requested at other times. The appointment of assistant surveyor went to William Crosley of Brighouse, whilst in 1793 Archibald Millar of Dublin was appointed resident engineer and superintendent.

The committee wasted no time in commencing the construction of the canal. The first contract, dated December 31st, 1792 was awarded to John Pinkerton, well known as a canal contractor, and John Murray of Colne. This was for the section from Ellel Grange to Tewitfield and was for £52,000, exclusive of bridges and culverts. The second contract, awarded in 1793, was for Ellel to Ray Lane near Catterall, making a total of 27 miles which, as experience was to show, was much too long a stretch.

In order to outflank the Leeds and Liverpool, it was essential to start work south of Preston and, in July 1793, the length from Bark Hill near Wigan to Adlington near Chorley was let to Paul Vickers of Thorne.

It was decided at the first annual sharholders' meeting in January, 1793 that communication with the sea was desirable, the outcome being Rennie's proposed branch from Galgate to Glasson Dock. This was authorised by a second Act of May 10th, 1793. This Act also imposed further restrictions on the drawing of water from the Lune, the Wyre and from mines near Heapey which were adjacent to the Leeds and Liverpool's parliamentary

Ellel Grange Bridge

line. Water, if required, was to be provided free elsewhere by mines within 2,000 yards of the canal, provided that it didn't have to be pumped from the pithead.

Negotiations were successfully concluded with the Duke of Bridgewater to extend the Lancaster Canal from Westhoughton to his own canal at Worsley, at a cost estimated by Rennie to be £63,544. A Bill authorising the connection was promoted in 1794 but lost, mainly owing to opposition by Miss Henrietta Atherton of Atherton Hall. The Duke decided to build a branch to Leigh and the Bill was not revived, the Lancaster committee feeling that the new branch might be more suitable for their junction in any case.

Meanwhile wrangling continued with the Manchester, Bolton and Bury and the Leeds and Liverpool committees over the latter's proposed deviation to the south of the Ribble. In October 1793 the Lancaster committee suggested that the Leeds and Liverpool join their line near Heapey, where both lines became parallel, which would have destroyed the Leeds and Liverpool's level to the Manchester, Bolton and Bury canal. In turn the Leeds and Liverpool counter-proposed that the Lancaster should strike south-eastwards, abandoning their own line and joining the Leeds and Liverpool at Newburgh. Access to the Bridgewater could then be from a branch of the Leeds and Liverpool at Wigan, attracting some Liverpool-Manchester traffic.

This second plan was not acceptable to the Lancaster committee, who were aware that their rival lacked funds, and was also opposed by the Duke of Bridgewater. Work on their south level had already been started and was supported by both the Duke and the Wigan coalowners. However a deviation was badly needed by the Leeds and Liverpool and to succeed they needed the backing of the Manchester, Bolton and Bury *and* the Lancaster. Inevitably a compromise with the Lancaster was reached. In April 1794, they agreed to support the deviation (and also the Manchester, Bolton and Bury's extension Bill) in return for support for a small deviation at Cabus, near Garstang, and the Worsley extension. There would now be two parallel lines, enabling the Leeds and Liverpool to link up with the Manchester, Bolton and Bury. Also, the Lancaster was to build a short connecting canal with the Leeds and Liverpool at Heapey to ensure that traffic would pass over their canal to the Bridgewater. If the junction was not built, there was the proviso that the Lancaster would pay the Leeds and Liverpool 1d per ton for all goods which would have passed through it on the way to Manchester, taking the shortest route. The Leeds and Liverpool's Bill was passed on May 9th, 1794 but, as has been seen, the Lancaster's was rejected.

Construction of the canal was proceeding whilst the various wranglings and negotiations took place, but not so quickly as it might have done. Pinkerton and Murray had not always been present to supervise the work as they were often attending to contracts on other canals. Not all the work was done by their own men, but various works were let to sub-contractors for the lowest possible price. Workmen were allowed to wander onto land which had not been purchased by the Lancaster Canal Company. Archibald Millar, the resident engineer, frequently complained of their inattention and bad workmanship. He found that Pinkerton and Murray ignored his instructions as soon as he had left an area, sometimes digging the canal yards from the line which he had laid.

During the building of the canal, various sections were completed and filled with water to enable boats to transport materials from one area to another. Once filled with water, it was not possible for Millar to check the puddle lining the canal to see that it had been properly made. Pinkerton and Murray objected to his wish to have those sections drained to be able to make his inspection.

In 1795 things came to a head between Millar and the contractors. Whitworth, the assistant surveyor, was called in to arbitrate. As a result the Lancaster Canal Company took over the disputed works in September and let them again as single lots under Millar's supervision. There were thirty-five contractors between Borwick and Preston, all having short stretches of perhaps two bridges or 500 yards of the line each. Millar was then able to supervise the construction of the canal to his satisfaction.

In their first detailed report published on August 30th, 1795 the committee reported that it was hoped to complete the Tewitfield to Ellel Grange section within two years, much of the masonry work on the bridges and aqueducts being well advanced. The section from Ellel Grange to the River Calder, it was hoped, would be completed in sixteen months, whilst the section on to Myerscough Wood should be completed in eighteen months. Nothing further appears to have been done north of the Ribble. To the south of the river, work was almost complete on the section from Limebrick Beck (near Chorley) to Bark Hill.

In 1794 Henry Eastburn had been appointed as resident engineer to the section south of the Ribble, with Thomas Fletcher assisting. Bark Hill to Adlington, 4.5 miles, was opened in 1795. Enough work had been done by July 1796 to allow a little coal traffic to commence earning some badly needed revenue.

The French Wars were causing hardship and restricting the flow of capital. Share calls were being ignored by some of the

Above: **The Preston terminus of the Lancaster Canal**

Below: **Cottam Hall Bridge, Preston, - a skew bridge**

shareholders and the company was heavily in debt with the treasurer's bank. An appeal for further subscriptions in advance met with little success, but a second appeal in 1797 was more forthcoming.

In May 1796, a third Act was obtained to authorise the purchase of some lands from the Duchy of Lancaster for a small deviation at Myerscough. During this same year plans for extending the line of the canal to Kendal were shelved and the Westmorland proprietors began to get restless (mainly because of the proposal to appropriate the statutory reserve of £60,000 reserved for the northern section in order to finance current work).

By now the Preston to Tewitfield section was almost completed, apart from the Lune aqueduct which was started in January 1794 but not completed until autumn 1797. More will be said about this magnificent structure later.

On November 22nd, 1797 the Lancaster Canal was formally opened from Spital Moss, just outside Preston, to Tewitfield. A cavalcade of six boats took part in the ceremony, but the actual voyage was only from Lancaster to the aqueduct and back. The order of proceedings was drawn up in great detail.

"The Committee meet in the office in Lancaster at 9.30 a.m. are to proceed from there, accompanied with colours and music, to the Canal Bridge in the Fryerage, where the boats must be placed ready to receive them in the following order.

Committee Barge. Committee, Leeds and Liverpool Committee and the most respectable of the landowners. The 'Bee' and 'Ceres' are to be fitted up for the particular friends of the Committee and the most respectable persons in Lancaster. Two of the trading boats belonging to the Company and the 'Elephant' are to be fitted up for the Proprietors in general and are to follow in order."

There is much more instruction including how, if the day be favourable, the notables may step out and view the aqueduct

Water lilies, buttercups and reeds,
looking towards BNFL, Salwick, nr Preston

whilst the boats were turning, the order of the boats for the return, where the band was to sail and the composition of the procession to the Kings Arms Hotel in Market Street Lancaster, to dine. Volleys were to be fired at various points, the final one in front of the town hall (which was then in Market Street).

In 1797 the 4 mile stretch from Adlington to Knowley Wharf, near Chorley, was opened. The balance sheet for the first six years gives details of the expenditure incurred during the construction of the Lancaster Canal.

Lancaster Level:

Land etc.	42,604-17-1^1/2	
General Expenditure	178,158-11-2	
Lune Aqueduct	48,320-18-10	
Hydraulic Pozzolano earth from Italy	321-8-9	269,405-15-10^1/2

Wigan Level:		
Land etc.	5,760-1-6	
General Expediture	55,416-16-3^1/2	61,176-17-9^1/2

Not particularly applicable to either part:

Applications to Parliament	6,327-1-2	
Salaries, fees etc.	16,341-11-9	
Quarrying, boat building and interest to proprietors	29,314-3-5	51,892-16-4
		£382,565-10-0

By 1799 William Cartwright was resident engineer to the Lancaster Canal Company, (he had been assistant resident engineer since January 1794) as Millar's and Eastburn's contracts were not renewed. He reported to the committee that the South End was completed from Bark Hill to Johnson's Hillock (12 miles) and that the remaining part to Clayton Green was well advanced, apart from the Whittle Hill's tunnel.

Until now the Company had suffered from financial difficulties, response from the proprietors having been poor; in July 1798 there was only £6,500 in the hands of the committee. However, a time of expansion now started, canalside industry continuing to grow until the railway era in the 1840's. On the North End the Company started a packet boat service in August 1798, between Preston and Lancaster, run by two boats which were to be paid for from their own earnings. By the second half of 1799 a total revenue of £2,022 was reported by the Committee. Samuel Gregson and three other committee members, trading as Samuel Gregson and Company, built lime-kilns at Preston and the Canal company opened up quarries. Between Bark Hill and Chorley in the following years new pits were opened, numerous lime-kilns were built at both ends of the canal, cinder ovens were built in the Tewitfield area (to provide a fluxing agent for the charcoal iron smelting of Lonsdale) and coke ovens were erected near Carnforth. There was coal traffic from small local pits in the Farleton area as well as from the mining areas at the southern end of the canal.

CHAPTER TWO:
RIBBLE PROBLEMS AND THROUGH TO KENDAL

By now the main problem was the connection of the two ends of the canal across the Ribble. Owing to bad roads at Johnson's Hillock, coal from collieries close to the South End near Wigan was being carted to the Douglas, sailed from there to Preston and then carted again to the North End. Various proposals were considered in 1796 and 1797 for a branch canal from the North End at Salwick to Savock, followed by an inclined plane down to the Ribble. An alternative was for a tramroad from Tulketh, nearer Preston, when traffic could then be exchanged with the Douglas, which the Leeds and Liverpool agreed to improve, but the Lancaster had insufficient funds for financing this work. Even more expensive was the building of an aqueduct which had been considered in 1794; Rennie estimated that the cost of a three-arched structure of 116 feet a span, plus embankments, was £94,979.

Cartwright was asked to make a survey and on November 1st, 1799 the committee issued a report of his findings. He said that the south level was intended to terminate at Clayton Green, the most northerly point before the commencement to the general fall to the vale of the Ribble. He estimated the cost of locking down 222 feet and then crossing the Ribble by an aqueduct at £180,945. Instead, as a cheaper and simpler method, he advised a double wagonway (one road for ascending and the other for descending wagons) to be hauled by a stationary steam engine. The river was to be crossed by a wooden bridge, then a similar wagonway was to be built to a proposed basin at Preston, requiring a short extension of the North End from Spital Moss. The estimated cost was £60,000. To finance this, and also to pay off the debts of the Company, a fourth Act of Parliament was obtained in 1800 which granted the power to raise an additional £200,000 in £30 shares.

Not all the monies were payable at once. An advert in the

Lancaster Gazette for June 20th, 1801 requests "respective proprietors of New Shares to pay Thomas Worswick £5 per share in cash or Bank of England notes before 1st July, 1801." A further £5 per New Share was called to be paid by October 1st, 1801.

A Mr Monk, who was probably a Leeds and Liverpool committee man, now came onto the scene with a further proposal to join the Leeds and Liverpool Canal. He considered Cartwright's tramroad good but expensive. His own suggestion was that the Douglas Navigation be continued from Rufford, via Tarleton Bridge and Bank Hall, to Penwortham where it would lock down to the Ribble. An inclined plane could be built up to the Lancaster from a basin in the opposite bank. At the South End there would be, of necessity, a connection between the Lancaster and the Leeds and Liverpool from Haigh to Wigan, this being by lock. This circuitous route, Monk estimated, would require an extra four hours time compared with Cartwright's tramroad when taking coal from Chorley to Preston. As compensation he suggested that the Leeds and Liverpool's tolls be reduced by 6d a ton.

As has been mentioned, a number of the Lancaster proprietors owned coal mines between Wigan and Chorley. One of them, Alexander Haliburton from Haigh, in a letter to George Clayton dated Febraury 25th, 1800, claimed that the scheme was a bait to the Lancaster's coal owners. He estimated that the Company would lose £54,100 in the first year and £10,750 annually thereafter if it was adopted, and was of the firm opinion that Cartwright's plan was preferable. His estimate was that a ton of coal delivered at Lancaster would cost 12/11 with Cartwright's plan, but 16/7 with Monk's. In conclusion he wrote that "the North End would be from thence supplied with a much greater proportion of the trade than has been calculated upon, and should it never go further, the views of the Company would be more amply fulfilled than by falling in with the insidious proposals of their Leeds and Liverpool rivals."

Not surprisingly, with the conflicting views, the committee asked John Rennie, their original engineer, and William Jessop to survey and give their opinion on the schemes. (Jessop was an experienced engineer of canals, having built a number particularly in the north-east and the midlands, who was completing the Rochdale Canal at the time. He also had practical experience in the building of tramroads.) Their report to the committee was presented to the General Meeting on July 7th, 1801. They said "We are still of the opinion that an embankment to the full height of the Lancaster level, and a Stone Aqueduct will be most advisable," this being together with locks up to Clayton Green. If the company was prepared to go to "extraordinary expense," the work could be done in three years, otherwise five. Attached to their report was a design for the aqueduct. It was to be built of stone, be 640 feet in length, have three elliptical arches with a span of 116 feet each and be 57 feet in height from the low water mark to the towing path. The cost was to be less than £94,979. There were two other designs for an aqueduct. One, from Cartwright, was for a slightly shorter aqueduct with three spans of 120 feet each which was to incorporate Corinthian pilasters. The other design, by Thomas Gibson, was for a continuous aqueduct with pointed arches, three of which were to span the Ribble. There were to be cross arches between the main spans and an immense pediment (a triangular piece with a long base). Rennie and Jessop, knowing that the Lancaster Canal Company did not have the funds available to build an aqueduct, approved Cartwright's tramroad, which it was estimated would cose £21,600, as a temporary measure. Owing to the advantage it would give to the Leeds and Liverpool they condemned the Douglas scheme. Cartwright's scheme for the building of the tramroad was immediately adopted and Jessop was retained to survey the Preston end of the line. For the work and the survey Jessop was paid £70, and £112-5s-4d was credited to Rennie's account.

No time was lost in starting the work which involved the cutting of the 259 yard tunnel through Whittle Hill to complete the line to Clayton Green, constructing a further mile of canal to Walton Summit which was the tramroad terminus, building the tramroad itself and extending the North End by half a mile into Preston. A basin was to be built to the north of Fishergate. Instead of the one year anticipated by Cartwright, it in fact took two years to bore the tunnel. On June 1st, 1803 the first boat passed through to Walton Summit where its cargo of coal was trans-shipped to tramroad wagons. However, the tramroad was only finished to Bamber Bridge and was not completed through to Preston until the end of the year. Its route skirted Avenham Brow, behind what is now Ribblesdale Place, and turned due north, passing under Fisher-gate to the wharf. The tramroad had a double track for ascending and descending wagons and three incline planes worked by stationary engines and endless chains, one of which rose from the then wooden trestle bridge in Avenham Park. Although this bridge over the Ribble has be rebuilt several times, it is still known as 'The Old Tram Bridge' today.

Shortly after the tramroad was completed, on January 19th, 1804, Cartwright died, probably as a result of overwork. During his time as an engineer to the Lancaster Canal he had planned and supervised the cutting of a tunnel from the canal at Preston, through the rock and out into the Ribble, the water being pumped to the canal by a Boulton and Watt steam engine. The work was completed by William Miller of Preston, an assistant engineer for some years, pumping commencing in July 1806.

Another of Cartwright's schemes had been taking water from the River Keer at Capernwray, using the wheel at Capernwray Mill to pump the water into the canal. In the event the pump was not built, owing to opposition from the mill owners, but a feeder from the river was cut. One of Cartwright's final designs was for a 2,200 yard tramroad from Tewitfield to the quarries at Kellet Seeds, but this, also, was not built.

The opening of the tramroad had an immediate effect on the Company's revenue. For 1803 gross income vas £4,853, whilst for 1804, after the tramroad opened it rose to £8,490. In 1803 a first dividend of $^1/2$% was declared. The second dividend declared was 1% in 1805; a rate that continued unchanged until 1825. (An analysis of revenue from 1807 is detailed on p.36.)

As the length of the South End, including the tramroad, was only 19 miles (compared with 42 miles for the North End to

Tewitfield) the major part of the traffic was clearly being discharged at Preston. So Preston began to assume a greater importance than Lancaster in the affairs of the canal, although it was still in the control of men from the latter town.

The Westmorland proprietors were by this time becoming justifiably restless because of the continued deferment of the completion of the line from Tewitfield to Kendal. At last, in 1805, the Company began considering the continuation of the canal. William Miller made surveys for two routes to Kendal: one was via Hincaster with a 340 yard tunnel through Hincaster Hill, the other was shorter but had a tunnel of 670 yards at Raines Hall, Sedgwick. As an alternative he suggested a 13 mile tramroad from Tewitfield which was to consist of three inclined planes (similar to that over the Ribble). The line was to ascend 70 feet at Tewitfield, then rise gradually for a further 10 feet to Crooklands, passing east of Lane Hill to Stainton. It was then to use Fletcher's line to the east of Stainton Hill, avoiding the gunpowder works, where it would ascend another 40 feet by an inclined plane to its highest level, then gradually descend 13 feet to Natland. At Natland it was to descend 32 feet by the final inclined plane to Natland Mill and proceed on to Kendal. The tramroad, it was estimated, would cost £38,574; the cheaper canal would cost about £71,755. Wakefield's gunpowder interests at Sedgwick influenced the committee who decided to adopt the Hincaster line, the canal to be 27 feet wide and 4.5 feet deep. This line virtually followed Whitworth's original line. On August 13th, 1807 their Bill for varying Rennie's line between Tewitfield and Hincaster and building tramroads to Farleton Knott and Kellet Seeds was passed. (This also permitted the construction of tramroads within the line of the canal, thus authorising, retrospectively, the building of the Preston tramroad.) The stipulation that the canal must be 7 feet deep from Kendal to Hincaster Green, and the provisions for taking water from the River Mint were, however, repealed. Water was to be abstracted from Stainton, Crooklands and Farleton becks instead.

A flight of eight locks at Tewitfield was to raise the level by 76 feet. The canal was to pass to the east of Holme, through Farleton and Crooklands to Stainton, where it was to turn west and pass beneath Hincaster Hill in a 378 yard tunnel and then turn northwards to Kendal. On February 7th, 1809 it was resolved that the work should commence. However, owing to the Napoleonic wars and a lack of funds, four more years were to elapse before construction started. Before then, in 1810, the committee bought 86 acres of land on Killington Common, five miles east of Kendal near the Sedbergh area fells. This was ready for a reservoir for the Kendal level.

1810 also saw the Lancaster committee reaching agreement with the Leeds and Liverpool over their use of part of the South End. The Lancaster was to construct seven locks at Johnson's Hillock, rising 64 feet to join with the Leeds and Liverpool line and a short extension from Bark Hill towards Wigan (which was already under construction). This did not mean that all squabbling ended, and in 1811 a serious dispute arose with twelve Leeds and Liverpool shareholders over alleged favouritism in the placing of contracts. Gregson and several of the committee men were accused of receiving favoured treatment in regard to their private business activities on the canal, and with their coal mining interests. Naturally a committee of investigation had to be appointed to look into these charges. In their report of August 7th, 1812 they not only found the accusations to be unfounded, but ended by praising Gregson and several of the committee members for their enterprise in setting up in 1797 as canal carriers to promote trade to the benefit of the Company. In addition they pointed out that Gregson had carried out duties far in excess of his office of clerk, and for no payment. "To his enterprize on the opening of the Canal, and to his subsequent indefatigable exertions, united with those of the Committee, may be attributed the progressive increase of the Tonnage Duties." In addition the committee were praised for raising money on their own securities when they could make no further calls on shareholders.

1812 saw the start of further activities for the completion of the 14.5 miles of line to Kendal. Thomas Cartwright was appointed engineer that year and instructed to make detailed estimates of the revenue potential and cost of the line. It was estimated that income would increase by a total of £7,589 per year (including £1,000 for the diversion of coastal trade from Milnthorpe to Lancaster and then on by canal), and £500 would be saved in the expense of pumping water at Preston owing to the amount which the locks would bring down. The cost of the extension was estimated at £98,095. At the end of the year it was resolved to begin work and the contract for making Hincaster Tunnel was let. Shuttleworth, one of the Preston proprietors, and several others put forward a scheme for crossing the Ribble on the level. At the same time as starting the Kendal line, Fletcher was asked to advise on this further scheme which he declared impracticable. Another scheme followed, which this time Fletcher agreed could be done although it would endanger water supplies. It was for a lower level aqueduct, involving more lockage on both sides. As it was estimated that it would cost £160,537, nearly twice the amount for the whole Kendal extension, there were obviously no funds available. At a Special General Meeting held in 1817, on Shuttleworth's demand, his resolution that an application be made for a loan from the Exchequer Bill Loan Commissioners was defeated.

Work was proceeding with both Hincaster Tunnel and Tewitfield Locks, the major engineering tasks on this section. The annual report to the General Meeting on February 7th, 1815 reveals the doubts and difficulties the committee had over the lining of the tunnel as, to them, brick was an inferior material to stone.

"The deep Cutting at both ends of Hincaster Tunnel is proceeding and the Excavation of the Tunnel is let. Much difficulty has arisen in endeavouring to procure stone for the Arching of this Tunnel. Limestone being the only stone within many miles of the work, and the quarries not yielding material of necessary dimensions, without very great expense, your Committee have some thoughts of arching the Tunnel with brick. From the opinions they have already taken (these investigations were in the Midlands) it does appear that

Junction Bridge and the junction with the main line, Galgate.
The Preston distance is to the present terminus
and not the original

Bricks have been generally used for Tunnels and the oldest Works in the Kingdom are formed with them, they have been found durable and the use greatly facilitates the execution. Within a short distance of the Tunnel (below Moss Side Farm near Heversham in fact), clay may be got - your Committee have procured some, and the bricks which have been made from it have the appearance of good and sound bricks and have met with the approbation of the engineers, who have seen them, and who have been accustomed to similar works. Your Committee are pursuing their enquiries and investigations respecting the nature of this clay, and should the result prove satisfactory, much time as well as expense will be saved in the execution on the Tunnel."

Twelve months later, the committee reported that the aqueduct over Stainton Beck and the Moss Lane Aqueduct were finished, and a considerable quantity of materials were laid down for those over Crooklands and Farleton becks. The masonry on one of the locks was complete whilst the others were in a state of forwardness. The deep cuttings at each end of Hincaster Tunnel were complete and one length of open cutting at the northern end complete. The southern end was ready for masonry as soon as the season would admit it. The first 10 yards at each end of the tunnel was to be lined with stone and the remainder with bricks, three hundred and fifty thousand of which had been made the previous summer. On February 4th, 1817 it was reported that two million bricks had been made and that half the tunnel was complete. On Christmas day the same year the tunnel was completed.

May 1817 saw William Crosley appointed independently of Fletcher to complete the work north of the locks and also the construction of Killington Reservoir.

On June 30th, 1817 the construction of the line from Hincaster to Kendal was publicly let. There were several navvies at the meeting and afterwards they caused considerable riot in the town. The *Westmorland Advertiser,* July 5th, 1817 claimed that sound policy demanded that the ruffians should be held up as an example to the unruly multitude which the cutting of the canal was to bring to the populous neighbourhood. By the end of 1818 the locks were completed; Fletcher was praised for their plan and the manner in which the workmanship was executed. By March 27th, 1819 the canal was filled with water to Crow Park (west of Natland) and by April 14th, the first boat came up to the Aynam Basin.

The official opening should have been held on May 1st, 1819 but was postponed owing to an embankment bursting 7 miles from Kendal. On June 18th, the canal was finally opened with all due ceremony. At 7.00 a.m. the gentlemen of the Kendal Town Corporation preceded by a band and a party of special constables, processed down the canal basin where they embarked on the Corporation barge, accompanied by a party of ladies. Another barge was filled with gaily attired occupants. All business had

*The double upper gates of the sea lock, the link between
the Lancaster Canal and Glasson Dock*

been closed in the town, flags had been hoisted and cannon were
fired from time to time. At 10.15 a.m., to the ringing of bells, the
flotilla set sail to Crooklands where they awaited the Lancaster
contingent, which included five trading boats of Messrs Hargreaves, Welch and Company and three packet-boats. The full
procession of sixteen boats then returned to Kendal, arriving at
the basin at 5.00 p.m. It was conjectured than ten thousand people
were on the side of Castle Hill awaiting the event. There followed
a dinner for one hundred and twenty at the town hall, with the
mayor presiding, and a ball in the Assembly Rooms. So, after
twenty-seven years in construction, the main line was complete
from Preston.

The completion of the canal had an immediate effect on Kendal.
Nicholson, (in the *Annals of Kendal,* 2nd edition, 1861) says:

"the spirit of improvement fully manifested itself in 1818

Thurnham Mill, lock 6 in the foreground Glasson Arm

and 1819. The date of the new town may, we conceive, truly be placed here at the time of the opening of the Lancaster and Kendal Canal. This event gave an impulse to the public spirit of the inhabitants and formed the commencement of a new era in the history of Kendal .... The old Miller's Close Bridge, which had stood since 1743, and was very narrow and ill adapted to the general medium of intercourse with the canal, was now thrown down and wholly rebuilt on a wider scale. The large warehouses and other buildings at the canal harbour, were all erected at this time; Kent Lane (which before was very steep, and so narrow that two carts could scarcely pass) was thrown open and the ascent considerably diminished; Long Pool was widened; Gandy Street erected; Kent Terrace and Castle Crescent were built shortly after. The Union Building Society commenced operations about this time; and

Brantbeck Bridge at the deep cutting near Lancaster

indeed on every side, numerous habitations were superadded to the town .... in a very short time the town assumed a new and modern appearance - so very different that any person having been absent for a few years, could scarcely have identified it."

Whilst the building of the canal extension was in progress, in 1818 the Kendal Town Corporation undertook the buiding of the basin, wharves and warehouses and Miller Bridge at a cost to them of £7,004-11s-6d. The expected income from the wharves and warehouses was £550 per annum but there were some expenses against this. The Lancaster Canal Company agreed, in return, to take the canal a few yards further on at Aynam.

The grounds where the canal ended were known as 'Tenter Grounds'. Tenters were frames, first of wood and later of wrought iron, that were fitted with sharp hooks at the top and bottom.

Processed woollen cloth was stretched on tenters to dry. There were 680 yards of tenters which had to be moved from Aynam and compensation of £227 was paid.

Killington Reservoir was constructed to feed the canal extension. As has been mentioned, the committee purchased 86 acres of land in 1810 ready for this work. It was completed by the time the Kendal section of the canal was opened. The embankment has been raised several times so that the reservoir now covers 153 acres and has a capacity of 4,000,000 cubic yards. It is one of the largest canal feeders in the country. Water is sent down Crooklands Beck as required, there originally being safeguards for the interests of mill owners on the beck. Not long after the reservoir was filled, a leak was discovered in the dam and the whole had to be drained to make the necessary repair. When this was done, forty cart-loads of fine red trout weighing 6-7 pounds each were caught and taken to Kendal market for sale.

Above: **The Glasson Arm of the Lancaster Canal from the lock at Thurnham Mill**

Below: **Operating the sea lock gates, which connect the Lancaster Canal Basin with the Dock, Glasson Dock**

CHAPTER THREE:
THE STABLE YEARS

The Lancaster Canal Company now sought their sixth and final Act of Parliament. The proprietors now wished to build the Glasson Dock branch (which had been authorised in the 1793 Act) in an endeavour to improve the fortunes of the Port of Lancaster and provide a link with the sea. More capital was required and so the Bill was drafted seeking the necessary powers. There was immediate opposition to the Bill, particularly from Preston where a canal crossing of the Ribble to make a through connection with the coalfields (thus eliminating the cost of carrying coal over the tramroad) was considered more important. In the *Preston Chronicle* it was observed that the Company had wasted enough money in "ornamenting the town of Lancaster with a grand aqueduct over the Lune, upon which the water had laid stagnant for over twenty years." The proposal to build a branch to Glasson Dock now in the hopes of reviving "the decayed port of Lancaster" was seen as an unfair indulgence. Once again, however, Lancaster had its way and the Act of Parliament was obtained on June 14th, 1819. Retrospectively it authorised both the building of Killington Reservoir and the connection at Johnson's Hillock with the Leeds and Liverpool, to which the 2/3 Toll under the 1792 Act was to apply. Powers were given to raise a mortgage of £270,000 on the tolls so as to finance work on the Glasson Dock branch and repay debts.

William Crosley was appointed superintendent of the entire canal in 1820. His estimate of the cost of the Glasson Dock branch was £34,608 and a decision to commence work on it was reached in 1823. Before reaching this decision, however, consideration was given to a connection with the sea at Hest Bank, the canal's nearest point to the sea, only a quarter of a mile from the foreshore.

Looking up the frozen canal from Bolton Turnpike Bridge, Bolton-le-Sands, Carnforth

There was a stone pier here, built in 1820, and goods were regularly trans-shipped from coastal vessels (particularly from Liverpool and Glasgow) for forwarding to Kendal by canal, then by road carrier to destinations such as Penrith, Kirkby Stephen and Hawes. In 1820 four vessels sailed from Liverpool every four or five days. Crosley estimated the cost of this linkage, including a dock (behind which was presumably the Hest Bank Shipping Company) at £69,591. At the time the Glasson decision was taken the Company resolved, probably to placate the shippers, that a drawback of 1/8 a ton on merchandise trans-shipped for Kendal at Hest Bank would be allowed. In anticipation of diverting trade from Preston and exporting coal from Glasson, Lancaster Port Commissioners, who were and are the owners of Glasson Dock, agreed to reduce their dues from 1/3 to 4d per ton for vessels passing through the branch. In return the Company paid the Port Commissioners £500, in two instalments, and guaranteed them a yearly income of £200 from ships from the Isle of Man, Ireland and beyond Galloway and Holyhead (trade from these areas then being of some size).

In December 1825, Crosley reported that the 2.5 mile Glasson branch was ready. However the usual cash shortage delayed the construction of warehouses and wharves, leading to slow growth in trade at first. Eventually a five-storey warehouse capable of dealing with 1,500 tons of goods at once was built. The commodious basin, having a depth of fourteen feet and covering 36,000 square yards, could take larger seagoing vessels as well as canal traffic.

The dividend payment for 1826 was raised to 1 1/2% in spite of the failure of Messrs Dilworth, Arthington and Birkett's bank, which lost the Company £4,500. Also as a result of the failure, a new treasurer had to be appointed. In 1828 the dividend was back to 1% again. Under the 1819 Act, mortgages of £134,550 had been raised and interest rates were rising, being 4% in 1825 and 5% in 1826. The Glasson Dock branch was opened on May 16th, 1826 with the passage through it of the sloop *Sprightly*, carrying a cargo of slate from the Duddon to Preston. It was August of the following year before the first vessel sailed through to Kendal. This was the 60-ton schooner *Seaforth* with a cargo of salt from Northwich. Both vessels were Preston registered.

In June 1826, the Glasson branch being open, Crosley resigned in order to take up the appointment of engineer to the Macclesfield Canal. He was succeeded by Samuel Gregson's son, Bryan Padgett Gregson, who had been assisting him since 1813 and was by now in charge of the canal's day-to-day management. He was particularly involved in the development of the packet-boat services running on the North End.

By 1823 the Canal Company had spent £600,000 on capital projects, which, of course, does not include the Glasson Branch. However, as recompense, both tonnage and gross income had risen steadily over the years (see below)

	South End & Tramroad		North End	Final Total
	Coal in Tons	**Total Tons**	**Total Tons**	
1813	90,000	109,000	113,000	222,000
1820	121,000	179,000	115,000	294,000
1825	215,000	303,000	156,000	459,000

Table 1
Increase in Tonnage Carried on the Canal between 1813 and 1825

(This is with the canal now open to Kendal)

Table 2
Income Generated by the Canal 1807-1823

	North End	South End	Packet-boats	Interest, Rents etc.	Total
1807	£6,181	£6,111	£818	£522	£13,632
1808	£7,015	£5,758	£300	£558	£13,631
1809	£7,154	£6,651	£478	£457	£14,740
1810	£7,758	£7,615	£602	£749	£16,715
1811	£8,572	£7,657	£793	£704	£17,726
1812	£9,039	£7,842	£445	£1,367	£18,693
1813	£9,501	£9,267	£572	£865	£20,205
1814	£8,913	£9,927	£749	£831	£20,420
1815	£8,264	£8,568	£477	£1,005	£18,314
1816	£8,406	£10,060	£310	£1,096	£19,872
1817	£7,589	£10,225	£184	£1,085	£19,083
1818	£9,268	£12,509	£232	£1,602	£23,611
1819	£11,140	£11,246	nil	£1,533	£23,919
1820	£12,803	£12,486	£43	£1,344	£26,676
1821	£11,875	£12,050	£590	£1,404	£25,919
1822	£11,696	£12,417	£630	£1,124	£25,867
1823	£12,870	£14,199	£247	£1,558	£28,874

The rise in income following the opening of the canal through to Kendal in 1819 will be noted.
(Figures provided from Baines' *Lancashire*.)

Glasson trade increased at the expense of Milnthorpe, Preston and Hest Bank, which finished as a port in 1831 when the Hest Bank Company transferred to Glasson. Milnthorpe, and later Sandside which became the port for Milnthorpe and was once known as Milnthorpe Sandside, declined as the port for Kendal and were finally made redundant in 1857 with the arrival of the

Ulverston and Lancaster Railway (the viaduct of which caused silting and changes in the Kent Estuary). The trade to the Lancaster quays remained comparatively stable, as did the town's growth for a time. However the coming of the canal and tramroad ensured that Preston flourished.

In 1804 the population of Preston was about 10,000, but by 1825 it had risen to over 30,000. The opening of the Glasson branch had helped foster the growth of the town, but it did little for the Ribble Navigation Company. The Ribble was difficult to navigate owing to sandbanks, silting and shifting channels. Imported goods were transferred to lighters off Lytham and landed at Preston quay at a cost of 14/10 per ton; the cost of importing to Preston via Glasson and the new canal was only 13/9 per ton and there was no need for smaller craft to trans-ship at Glasson. In 1829 the Ribble Navigation Company stated that "Scotch and Foreign trade vessel have left the port for the superior advantages of Glasson." Eventually, in 1838, a new company was formed to take measures to restore trade to the Ribble.

In 1830, 16,036 tons passed through Glasson Dock, the bulk of it continuing on to the canal. In the same year sixty-four ships carrying 4,633 tons passed over the canal from Glasson from the £200 guarantee area. By 1840 these figures had risen to one hundred and eighty-five ships carrying 12,128 tons. (In addition there must have been other ships from within the guarantee area which sailed up the canal, but these cannot be identified with certainty.) Trade outwards was coal to North Wales, Ireland and Ulverston; inwards it was mainly slate, timber, grain and potatoes.

1827 saw a final scheme to unite the Lancaster with the Leeds and Liverpool canals via the Douglas published by Twyford and Wilson, civil engineers and surveyors from Manchester. Their Ribble crossing was to be by wooden booms moored across the river from the mouth of the Douglas to Freckleton, forming a floating towpath. Two navigation channels were to be left in the middle; on the crossing of these the authors were significantly silent! A new canal from Freckleton was to rise by 79 feet 4 inches via ten locks and join the Lancaster near Salwick. From it, another canal would be made crossing the Fylde to Thornton via Kirkham and Poulton-le-Fylde. A harbour was proposed at Thornton, further up the Wyre than Fleetwoood which became a port in its own right twenty-two years later having originally been opened under Preston in 1840. This scheme would have seen the end of the hindrance of the Lancaster's tramroad and brought trade from cargoes of grain to be carried from the Fylde. It was estimated that the 11.25 miles of new canal would cost under £80,000. Neither the Lancaster nor the Leeds and Liverpool took any interest in the scheme.

By this time the shadow which was to be cast over the Lancaster Canal and others, and which would eventually lead to their demise as commercial waterways, was already on its way - the railway era was about to begin.

CHAPTER FOUR:
THE COMING OF THE RAILWAYS

In 1831 the Wigan and Preston Railway was authorised, a line running roughly parallel to the canal but some distance away. In a report dated July 20th, 1830, during the promotion of the line, B.P.Gregson put forward four alternative suggestions to meet this danger to the canal. The first was the conversion of the tramroad into a railway in order to speed the trans-shipment of goods. The second was the same, but with suitable deviations to permit its being worked by locomotive. The third was the possibility of amalgamation with the railway and the abolition of the tramroad. The final alternative was to abolish the tramroad, leaving the South End for the sole use of the Leeds and Liverpool and so forcing the railway to make branches to the pits on the canal. Gregson realised that railways were here to stay and pointed out that if the Canal Company opposed the Wigan and Preston Railway, another scheme would soon take its place. The pattern of trade was bound to change and the Company should accept the fact. Gregson felt that if the committee were to insist on opposing the railway, the most effective method of doing so would be to promote one of their own instead.

The committee decided to look into the first alternative and apppointed George Stephenson to investigate the possibility of the tramroad conversion. His recommendation was for two diversions and four self-acting inclines, the existing engine-worked incline from the bridge over the Ribble being retained. In his report to the committee Gregson said "I cannot but consider Mr Stephenson's plan attended with many difficulties and inconveniences, not only in execution, but even in operation." The cost of the plan was estimated to be £11,895.

These were the days of railway mania and more lines were being promoted - for example, Manchester to Bolton and Bolton to Preston via Chorley were two such, of consequence to the canal. Where it was advantageous, the Lancaster's policy was to compete, otherwise it co-operated. In 1834 the North Union Railway, of which the Wigan and Preston had become a part, opened its main line through to Preston and also a branch line from Wigan to New Springs. The branch crossed the line, authorised by Parliament, of the Lancaster Canal to Westhoughton. It did so at a point just beyond the junction with the Leeds and Liverpool Canal at Wigan Top Lock. As a result, in 1836 the Lancaster Canal Company hastily extended their line a few hundred yards towards Westhoughton so as to force the railway to build a bridge. Since the Company had abandoned all hopes of completing their line by then, this extension was useless. Its purpose was to make the North Union Railway, who had refused agreement to a protective clause being included in their Bill, realise that they could not ride roughshod over the canal.

The Bolton and Preston Railway's line, however, followed the canal so closely that the Company was forced to reach an agreement with them. The railway company also wanted to use the tramroad route to gain entry to Preston. An agreement was reached in January 1837 whereby the tramroad was leased to the railway in perpetuity, together with land for a station to be built near the Preston basin. The railway was to receive all tolls from the South End traffic other than those from the Leeds and Liverpool. In exchange the railway's promoter agreed to pay the Company a rent of £8,000 per annum and construct a short transfer siding from their Preston terminus to the canal basin. A locomotive was to be reserved exclusively to operate the trans-ferred traffic between the Canal Company's North End and South End. In July 1837 the railway company obtained their Act, and a year later they obtained a second one which authorised them to enter Preston over the North Union's metals from Euston, thus leaving them saddled with a tramroad which they no longer required. Not surprisingly the Lancaster Canal Company had no desire to take it back. Eventually the railway agreed to maintain the tramroad for the Canal Company's use at a reduced rental of £7,400, thus allowing for the expense of the upkeep. Later the rental was reduced to £7,000 by the Company itself, rather than

Looking towards the lock keeper's cottage, Galgate

allow the benefit of preferential coal rates go to the railway company for traffic transferred at Preston to the North End.

Gregson foresaw that the railways would build branches to the collieries and gradually take over the canal's coal traffic, so he therefore advised disposing of the tramroad when the opportunity arose. In 1865 he explained that "The result otherwise would have been the loss of nearly the whole of that Traffic and a considerable outlay in repairs. This agreement also secured and improved the Coal Traffic of the North End by connection with the North Union and the Bolton and Preston Railway at Preston." By concentrating on the North End, with its long established trade, through the newly built transfer sidings at Preston, the Company gained cheap supplies of coal which they were able to export through Glasson.

Meanwhile, other events were taking place. 1836 saw the Ribble pumping engine and land sold because Killington Reservoir had

Junction Bridge and Lock 1, Galgate

proved itself to be adequate in supplying the canal. Following two collapses in 1827, with a third in 1836, the Whittle Hill Tunnel was opened out in the middle in 1838 in order to form two separate short tunnels.

In 1837 a Bill proposing the inevitable railway to Lancaster, the Lancaster and Preston Junction Railway, was put before Parliament. The Company objected to the Bill as the proposed line, crossing "the Canal Company's Wharfs, west of the Canal in Preston, will deprive them of an indispensable portion of their ground and prevent the extension of conveniences and facilities, absolutely necessary in the formation of a Basin, Coal Yard and Wharfs." They wished a clause to be inserted in the Act to prevent the railway company from entering upon any of their land or property without their consent. The eventual outcome was that some land at Dock Street was sold to the railway company.

The construction of a ship canal from Lytham Pool to Marsh Lane in Preston had been proposed in the 1830's. As this would have been separate from the Lancaster by only 600 yards, there had been talk of connecting the two. Nothing came of the scheme.

During this time of change and uncertainty, trade had still continued to grow, reaching the peak year for the whole canal in 1840 (see below).

The year 1837 saw the dividend rising to 1.25% whilst in 1840 it was $1^7/20$th%. Repayment of mortgages was also continuing steadily. However, June 1840 saw the opening of the railway to Lancaster, an event which was to have unusual repercussions on the future of the Lancaster Canal.

Table 3 Increase in Tonnage and Revenue on the Canal between 1836 and 1840					
	South End & Tramroad		North End	Final Total	Revenue
	Coal in Tons	Total Tons	Total Tons		
1836	251,000	377,000	173,000	550,000	£33,000
1840	291,000	424,000	193,000	617,000	£34,200

CHAPTER FIVE:
THE CANAL AND THE LANCASTER AND PRESTON JUNCTION RAILWAY

It is useful at this point to turn to the history of the Lancaster and Preston Junction Railway, which came to be the Lancaster Canal's major competitor.

The Lancaster and Preston Junction Railway which opened on June 25th, 1840 had an end-on junction with the North Union at Preston. The two had a joint working agreement and shared the station, although agreement to this had been reached with difficulty. Three weeks later the Preston and Wyre Railway, which also had use of the North Union station, was opened to Fleetwood. It became a competitor with the Lancaster and Preston Junction for Scottish traffic when a steamer service to Ardrossan was opened in May 1841.

The Lancaster Canal Company halved their fares (see Chapter Nine) between Lancaster and Preston on the opening of the railway, and continued to carry roughly the same number of passengers as before, probably helped by several minor accidents on the railway which caused delays to traffic. In June 1841 the North Union gave the Lancaster and Preston notice of termination of their joint working agreement on December 31st. Agreement was reached with the Bolton and Preston Railway that their Preston station would be completed and that the Lancaster and Preston would have use of it from January 1st, 1842. The North Union then protested that the termination of the agreement was not intended to cover the use of their station, and a bitter quarrel between the companies developed this which resulted in inconvenience to passengers, some of whom used the canal instead.

The opening of the Bolton and Preston line was delayed owing to construction difficulties at the tunnel and cuttings near Chorley, and this meant less traffic than anticipated for the Lancaster and Preston Junction. Also, rather than carrying on to Lancaster,

*Looking along the Lune Aqueduct to Bulk Aqueduct from
the Halton Road Bridge, Lune Aqueduct Open Day, 25.11.89*

it had become more convenient to use the Preston Wharf to transfer northern traffic to the Canal directly. As a result of all this, takings fell short of expectations and the railway company found itself in financial difficulties. The Lancaster and Preston Junction Railway, panic-stricken, sought a purchaser, but their terms were not acceptable to either its friend the Bolton and Preston, or to the North Union. They next sought a deal with the Lancaster Canal Company, who seized their chance and reversed the more usual procedure of railways purchasing canals. On September 1st, 1842 they took a twenty-one year lease on the railway.

The Company was to pay a rent of £13,300 per annum (which represented a 4% dividend) and take on the interest payments on the £113,000 which had been borrowed by the railway company. Moreover the Company undertook not to oppose the projected railway to Carlisle and if the line was completed within the twenty-one years, to agree to an increase in the rental. An Act of Parliament empowering the lease was passed on April 3rd, 1843. At that time there were two schemes mooted for lines between Lancaster and Carlisle; one for a line via Kirkby Lonsdale that went up the Lune Valley, the other for a line via Kendal. Naturally the Lancaster Canal Company favoured the former as it would not be in direct competition with them, and they even promised to invest £50,000 in the scheme. However, they were forced to withdraw their offer so as to buy off opposition to the railway company's leasing bill.

The Manchester, Bolton and Bury had worked the Lancaster and Preston Junction line by an earlier agreement. On the Lancaster Canal Company's acquisition of that railway's locomotives, the arrangement was continued by a new agreement which also provided for the engines to work to Bolton. The North Union had wished to enter a joint agreement for the Preston - Manchester traffic, an offer which was rejected and which resulted in bitter competition between them and the Bolton and Preston until the amalgamation of the two companies on January 1st, 1844. This amalgamation forced the Lancaster Canal Company to reach an agreement with the North Union and it started using their station again from February 13th, 1844.

By this time the Lancaster and Carlisle Railway plans had taken shape, the route via Kendal having been chosen. The new railway company quickly reached a provisional agreement with the Company whereby the latter would manage the North End and the Glasson branch for and on behalf of the railway company for a guaranteed income of £11,000 per annum. As the canal's receipts for the second half of 1843 totalled £10,223, the Company evidently anticipated that there would be a considerable fall in revenue on the opening of the railway. The Company offered the Lancaster and Carlisle Railway an option on the remaining years of the lease of the Lancaster and Preston Junction at £1,250 per annum, stone from the Company's quarry at Lancaster for use in constructing the line and general assistance in building the railway. However, as usual, disagreement arose, this time over the inclusion in the agreement of the wharves at Preston. The Company therefore opposed the Lancaster and Carlisle's Bill, but in June 1844 the railway was authorised.

By this time reasons had been found for believing that the lease of the Lancaster and Preston Junction Railway to the Lancaster Canal Company was illegal. The Act of 1843 only gave powers for the lease and did not refer to the terms which had been agreed upon. The draft of the lease, although it was supposed to have taken effect from September 1st, 1842, was not presented to the railway company until 1843 when it was found to contain clauses permitting a sub-lease. No doubt this was to permit sub-leasing of the railway to the Lancaster and Carlisle, which had now been approved. The railway company objected to this, as they too were interested in leasing their line to the new Lancaster and Carlisle Railway. Subsequent negotiations with the Lancaster Canal Company were unsuccessful so that in October 1844 the two railway companies considered themselves free to come to terms by themselves. The Lancaster and Preston was leased to the Lancaster and Carlisle from September 1st, 1846.

Before continuing with the saga of the Lancaster and Preston Junction Railway, other events in the life of the Lancaster Canal should be brought up to date. The Canal Company worked the railway very successfully from their own point of view, but not in the eyes of its users. Their first act on acquiring the railway had been to withdraw the packet-boats between Preston and Lancaster, at the same time increasing the fares by train and removing the seats from the third class coaches to make room for more passengers. A letter from 'Not a Well-wisher to Tub-travelling, but to the Public at Large', appeared in the *Lancaster Guardian* in 1843, complained at having to pay 2/6 to travel to Preston and only be able to sit on the floor with a good chance of being trodden on! When the trains stopped, he complained, all the passengers were jostled together. Another complaint against the Canal Company during that period was that, on one train, second class passengers not travelling through to Birmingham and London were also conveyed in a third class carriage.

In 1845 Hargreaves and Son ceased carrying merchandise on the railway, leaving the Lancaster Canal Company with an absolute monopoly of all passenger and freight traffic over both railway and canal. This they exploited, making a profit of £5,000 from the railway in 1845 which was then considerably increased in each of the following years. Strange to relate, most of the blame from the public for the way the railway was run was laid at the Lancaster and Preston Junction's door, not the Canal Company's.

Glasson Dock continued to thrive until 1846, when trade started to fall. There was by now a challenge from Fleetwood (to where the Preston and Wyre Railway line had been opened) and, with ships growing in size, the difficulties of entering Glasson increased because of the sandbanks in the Lune Estuary. Improvements on the Ribble posed a further threat to Glasson. As has been mentioned, a new company was incorporated in 1838 to cut a new and deeper channel up the river, to enlarge the quay at Preston and build a dock at Lytham where large ships unable to pass up the river could discharge their cargoes into lighters. This scheme was completed in 1842, and a branch railway opened in 1846.

To combat this, three new schemes were put forward in Lancaster in the 1840's. One was Stephenson's scheme to improve the river by deepening the channel to the Lancaster quays. Another scheme was for the construction of a new dock at Thornbush (which had been the site of a scheme in 1799) with a railway to the Lancaster and Preston Junction line at Ellel. The third, and most seriously considered scheme was for docks to be constructed at Poulton Ring (now Morecambe), these being connected to the Lune at Lancaster by a ship canal 3.5 miles in length across the peninsula to the river where a dam would maintain deep water at the quays.

Edmund Sharpe, a Poulton landowner who was also an engineer and architect, proposed this scheme. He was the secretary of the 'little' North Western Railway whose line from Skipton was originally planned to terminate at Lancaster. The intention was that an improved port at Lancaster would further trade between the West Riding of Yorkshire and the west coast. Capital was available for financing one of the schemes because in order to secure Admiralty consent to bridge the Lune, the Lancaster and Carlisle had paid £16,000 compensation to Lancaster merchants and £10,000 for improvements to the river. When in 1845 the Tidal Harbours Commission held an enquiry into the best method of utilising the £10,000, Sharpe attacked the Thornbush scheme as being yet another blow to the Port of Lancaster from the Lancaster Canal Company who already monopolised the town's communications through being lessees of the Lancaster and Preston Junction Railway. On behalf of the 'little' North Western Railway, backed by the Midland Railway and so-called to distinguish it from the London and North Western Railway, Lancaster merchants and Poulton landowners (including Sharpe) went on to press for the ship canal scheme. Both the Lancaster Canal and the Lancaster and Carlisle Railway opposed it as they considered that it would be severely prejudicial to the future of Glasson Dock.

The Morecambe Bay Harbour Company was floated shortly afterwards with a view to building a harbour and making a ship canal to Lancaster. When their formal prospectus came out in November 1845 it was found that a railway had been substituted for a canal, which had been reluctantly given up owing to the anticipated cost of construction. It was estimated that a canal would have cost £50,000 more than had originally been anticipated, thus having adverse effect on shipping charges. Sharpe said that the opposition from the Lancaster and Carlisle had not been anticipated and, as they were giving the £10,000 for the improvements to the Lune, their opposition would carry weight in Parliament. Whilst there was some agitation from Lancaster for a canal, it was short-lived and, in 1846, the Morecambe Harbour Railway Act was passed having received but little opposition. Later in the year the company was purchased by the 'little' North Western, exercising their option to do so. With the £10,000 from the Lancaster and Carlisle Railway the Lune was deepened, but this was only a temporary improvement and gradually the port at Morecambe took most of the trade. The Midland Railway, who had in turn taken over the 'little' North Western, transferred its shipping activities to the new port at Heysham in 1904.

Discussions between the Lancaster and Carlisle Railway and Lancaster and Preston Junction Railway Companies had continued and, by the end of 1845, the two boards had agreed that an amalgamation should take place immediately. The threat from the 'little' North Western Railway had helped precipitate this as their line from Skipton (where they had a junction with the Midland Railway) to Lancaster and Morecambe was considered by the Lancaster and Preston Junction to be a threat to their own line. Agreement had been reached with the Canal Company allowing it to pass under the Lune Aqueduct. The 'little' North Western Railway was incorporated in 1846.

In February 1846 an extraordinary general meeting was held and the directors of the Lancaster and Preston Junction put their proposals to the shareholders for ratification. However, the shareholders felt that better terms could be obtained by waiting until the Lancaster and Carlisle had been built and the Preston - Lancaster traffic had increased. An amendment to the effect that the proposed merger be not carried out received the unanimous support of the shareholders. All but one of the directors (he was not present at the meeting) thereupon resigned. The meeting had no power to appoint a new board as, under their Act, they could only elect three new shareholders to the board at the annual general meeting each June: the quorum was five directors, thus it would be two years before a board would be able to hold a meeting once again.

The railway was now theoretically legally leased to the Lancaster and Carlisle, but in practise it was illegally leased to the Lancaster Canal Company. The Lancaster and Carlisle demanded that the Company surrender the line on July 1st, 1846, but they refused to do so, continued running trains as before and started Chancery proceedings against the Lancaster and Preston Junction, seeking an injunction for the enforcement of the lease of 1842.

On September 22nd, 1846 the Lancaster and Carlisle Railway was opened between Lancaster and Kendal. Cheekily, they ran six trains a day through to Preston over the Lancaster and Preston Junction's metals (to which they had constructed a link from their Lancaster Castle Station despite opposition from the Company), without authority and in the face of great protests. The Company also ran local trains between the two towns and on the opening of the line to Kendal, promptly withdrew their Lancaster - Kendal packet-boat services.

The Lancaster and Carlisle Railway added insult to injury by sending statements of their traffic over the Lancaster and Preston Junction line but refusing to pay tolls, claiming that they considered there was no legally constituted body to which they could be paid!

However, the Canal Company had another trick up its sleeve. February 1847 saw the East Lancashire Railway offering to buy both the canal and the Lancaster and Preston Junction Railway. £29,000 outright was to be paid for the railway and the canal was to be purchased for £23,500 per annum, this being redeemable within ten years at twenty-five years' purchase. Agreement was almost reached, but both parties withdrew after the shareholders of the Lancaster and Preston Junction appointed a new, illegal board of directors to consider the proposal. Then once again the Canal Company tried to enforce the 1842 lease granted by the 1843 Act, but this was summarily dismissed by the railway shareholders who proceeded with their own arrangements for the leasing of the line. The Lancaster and Preston Junction shareholders held a general meeting on November 4th, 1847 when they unanimously rescinded their 1843 agreement to the lease. Committees were then appointed by both the Railway and Canal companies to meet and have discussions on the situation. The Lancaster and Preston Junction was determined not to lease to the canal; the Lancaster Canal Company said that it was prepared to dispose of its interest in the railway on payment of adequate compensation. At this time the Company also required support in the execution of their 1844 lease and recovery of tolls from the Lancaster and Carlisle Railway. The Lancaster and Preston Junction refused to lend their support and, in retaliation, the

Canal Company withheld its half-yearly rent payment due on March 1st, 1848. Each then took legal proceeding against the other to enforce what they considered to be their legal rights.

The Lancaster Canal Company, who in spite of the dispute over tolls were still on comparitively friendly terms with the Lancaster and Carlisle, then turned to that railway company with their rent proposals. They would sell the canal to the railway company outright together with the Lancaster and Preston Junction Railway for 38/- per share plus 5% per annum in perpetuity on payment of the outstanding tolls, the amount of which was still being negotiated. The Lancaster and Carlisle then counter-offered 30/- per share, subject to their taking over the Company's suit in Chancery against the Lancaster and Preston Junction and successfully obtaining it. This offer was accepted by the Canal Company, but fell through later due to the Lancaster and Carlisle's desire to make subsequent unacceptable changes.

On August 21st, 1848 the farce of two companies each running its own trains over the line ended in inevitable tragedy. On that day the 9.00 a.m. Euston to Glasgow express was running one hour fifteen minutes late when, hauled by "Dalemain," a Lancaster and Carlisle engine, it rounded the curve at Bay Horse. Ahead, too late to pull up, the driver Richard Morris saw a Lancaster and Preston train still standing in Bay Horse station; he ran into its rear, fatally injuring a passenger.

An enquiry under Captain Laffan R.E. of the Board of Trade followed. He found that the signalling on the line was bad, one small red flag on a staff at each station. Among the other causes of the crash he found "The uncertainty as to who is the rightful possessor of the line" and "The want of a proper understanding between the Lancaster and Carlisle and the Lessees of the Lancaster and Preston Junction Railway." Captain Laffan also suggested that the two companies "should come to a good understanding and that every effort should be made to determine the right ownership of this railway."

The Railway Commissioners instructed the Lancaster and Preston to set their house in order. October 1848 saw a committee of directors appointed to reach agreement with the Lancaster Canal Company. Agreement was reached on Novermber 13th, 1848 and ratified in December 1848 by a special meeting of the canal proprietors. The Company was to be paid £4,875 per annum for the unexpired portion of the twenty-one year lease, with an option to consolidate the full sum plus 5% within the first eighteen months, or 4.5% thereafter during the fifteen-year term. The injunction proceedings instigated by the Company were to be withdrawn, each side paying its own costs. The Lancaster and Preston Junction was to promote a Bill seeking parliamentary sanction for itself. If the Bill failed, they agreed that they would ratify the 1842 lease to the Lancaster Canal Company. The Act which was passed in 1849 went further. Independent agreement had been reached between the Lancaster and Preston Junction and the Lancaster and Carlise that the former be joined with the latter on a profit-sharing basis. The Lancaster Canal Company had to give up possession of the Lancaster to Preston line from the passing of the Act, and it did so on August 1st, 1849. The Lancaster and Carlisle was ordered to pay to the Company the outstanding tolls, the terms to be settled by arbitration. Robert Stephenson was the appointed arbitrator and he awarded the canal £55,551-10s-7^{1}/2d.

Overall, the Lancaster Canal Company came out of the seven years' wrangle very well. They had a profit of £67,391 which enabled them not only to pay off their outstanding mortgages of £26,000, but also to give a £1-17s-6d per share bonus to each proprietor and set up a £6,700 contingencies fund.

Compared with other canals, the Lancaster's dividends were consistently low, being 2% in 1845, 2^{1}/2% in 1846, 2^{1}/4% in 1847 and 1848 and then dropping back again to 2% in 1849 and 1850. Glasson trade continued at a fairly steady level from the £200 guarantee area, being £227-15s-1d in 1846, £219-10s-0d in 1847, £282-8s-9d in 1848, £249-18s-0d in 1849 and £281-13s-4d in 1850. However, the number of vessels over the arm was falling, being only twenty-three from the £200 guarantee area.

Matters would have been much worse if the canal had still been running the tramroad. From 1840 traffic over it declined, partly owing to the Bolton and Preston increasing the tolls. In 1839 there was a net profit of about £1,000 from the South End tolls and tramroad. This was after paying for rent, heavy repairs and maintenance from a gross income of £10,000. By 1850 the North Union Railway, who had acquired the Bolton and Preston, were showing a loss of about £5,600, having received a revenue of only £1,700.

The Lancaster Canal Company fixed P.B.Gregson's salary at a minimum of £1,000 per annum for the rest of his service in recognition of his negotiations with the railway company on their behalf in 1844. In 1846 he accepted the management of the Edinburgh and Glasgow Railway whilst continuing to work for the Canal Company at his full salary. Both employers were agreeable to his dual role. In October 1846 his father, Samuel Gregson, died at the age of eighty-three after fifty-four years' service. He had assumed duties far beyond those for which the Company paid him in an endeavour to promote its prosperity. He was highly respected in Lancaster, where he was twice made mayor. On Samuel's death, B.P.Gregson succeeded him in the appointment of clerk.

In 1850 a traffic sharing agreement was reached between the Lancaster and Carlisle Railway and the Lancaster Canal Company whereby the former carried the passenger and merchandise traffic to Kendal, and the latter retained the coal and heavy goods traffic as well as the traffic between Glasson Dock, Preston and elsewhere. (For destinations beyond Kendal, coal rates were subject to negotiations.) The reaching of this agreement reveals that the Lancaster Canal Company was still a powerful force in north Lancashire although, by this time, railway companies had taken control of several of the other canals.

CHAPTER SIX:
THE LAST YEARS OF THE LANCASTER CANAL COMPANY

In 1845 the Lancaster offered to 'sell' the South End outright to either the Lancaster and Carlisle Railway or the Leeds and Liverpool Canal. Subsequently an offer was made to the Leeds and Liverpool alone at a price of £7,000 per annum for the first three years and £6,300 per annum thereafter. (Included in the offer were the locks at Johnson's Hillock and the Anglezarke land.) Not surprisingly, the Leeds and Liverpool declined this offer, but in 1850 they leased all the merchandise tolls of the South End for £4,335 per annum for a twenty-one year term. They had to do this to counter a lawsuit by the Lancaster Canal Company, and the agreement was ratified at a special general meeting of the Lancaster Canal Company in October 1851.

Around this time there were abortive negotiations with the Kendal and Windermere Railway for a tramroad from the canal head to the proposed Kendal station. 1851 saw a proposal for another tramroad, which was to expand the canal's traffic, connecting Kendal to Staveley, Birthwaite (now Windermere) and other parts of the Lake District. Nothing came of the scheme and this meant that coal still had to be carted between the canal head and Kendal railway station.

Competition from the Lancaster and Carlisle was by now having an effect on the Glasson trade. In an effort to counter this, long-term contracts were entered into for the carriage of coal at reduced rates and, in February 1851, the Company resolved to engage in coastal traffic. Eight vessels, not all in use at the same time, are supposed to have been owned by the Company, but the entries of ships at Glasson show only five. The first vessel to be purchased was the schooner *Woodbine,* which was followed by the *Richard* in 1852. The *Richard* was shortly lost in the Duddon. Next the *Oriental* was purchased and then, in 1853, the *Bloomer* and three more ordered in 1855. Also in 1855 a screw steamer, the *Dandy,* was tried on the canal. Coal trade with Ireland had grown to such an extent that the Company rented a quay at Belfast and appointed an agent there. However, the boost to the Glasson revenue was only temporary and the gradual decline, which had started in 1850, continued. Figures in the £200 column of the Lancaster Port Commissioners' Registers show £281-13s-4d for 1850, £253-10s-5d for 1851, £181-5s-4d for 1852, £181-14s-4d for 1853, £225-3s-4d for 1854, £141-9s-3d for 1855, £201-9s-8d for 1856 and £194-0s-8d for 1857. In 1856 the four vessels' voyages at Glasson totalled 4,732 tons. Even though returns had dropped below £200, the Port Commissioners never received the difference to make up the £200 guarantee. In 1853, the Canal Company was reported to the Lancaster and Carlisle for importing pig iron and treacle from Greenock and Glasgow through Glasson to Preston for Blackburn and east Lancashire. These goods were being carried at very low rates so as to compete with transport by sea to Fleetwood and Preston. It was felt that the carriage of these goods could be a contravention of the agreement with the railway company and so the Canal Company opened their books for the Lancaster and Carlisle's inspection. The latter raised no objection, even though the report of the jointly appointed referee stated that technically there could have been an infringement. 1856 saw the books inspected again without dispute. However, in September 1858 the Lancaster and Carlisle served notice of its intention to terminate the competition agreement owing to the canal's violation through their carriage of treacle and pig iron. Incidentally, the treacle and iron trade seems to have disappeared after 1860, presumably taken over by the railway.

In May 1856 the Lancaster and Carlisle had leased the short line of the Kendal and Windermere Railway. Upon its acquisition they started to impede the Canal Company's coal supply to the Lake District, encouraging transport to Windermere by rail instead. With old agreements thus disregarded, the Canal Company started new negotiations, but these were broken off by the Lancaster and Carlisle who refused to come to terms whilst the canal

Looking up the drained canal from Bolton Turnpike Bridge

continued with the Glasgow traffic in treacle and iron.

By this time, as a result of amalgamations, the London and North Western Railway controlled all the West Coast route to the south of Preston and had an interest in the Lancaster and Carlisle, whose line they had helped to finance and whose board included seven of their own directors. The London and North Western were noted for their lack of friendly co-operation with rivals, canals in particular, and in 1857 they leased the Lancaster and Carlisle outright.

As a result of this change in ownership, the Lancaster Canal Company had to turn elsewhere to acquire traffic. July 1859 saw the steamer *Duchess,* the Lancaster Steam Navigation Company's vessel, begin twice-weekly sailings carrying merchandise between Glasson and Liverpool at a hire charge of £37-10s-0d per trip. Steam tugs were tried on the canal and in June 1860 the company purchased two second-hand ones to join the specially built existing one which was already at work. However, the coasting vessels were steadily being lost at sea until, in 1861, the *Woodbine* was the only one left. Trade continued to be poor, the dividend remained constant at 1.75% from 1851 until 1862 when it dropped to £1-13s-6d, then to £1-12s-0d in the following year.

In September 1860 the first moves to sell out to the London and North Western Railway seem to have been made. Negotiations proceeded for over two years before terms were agreed and a Bill was promoted in 1863. It successfully passed through the Commons, but the Lancashire and Yorkshire Railway opposed its passage through the Lords because it had a part interest in the tramroad (owing to their being joint lessees of the North Union with the London and North Western) and wished to participate in the lease of the canal. The London and North Western objected to this and withdrew their Bill, but reintroduced it in the next session. Passage was successful and on July 29th, 1864 the Bill received Royal Assent. Under the Lancaster Canal Transfer Act the London and North Western Railway was authorised to lease the North End in perpetuity for £12,665-17s-6d per annum, whilst the Leeds and Liverpool Canal Company were authorised to lease the South End for £7,075 from July 1st. There were to be increased maximum tolls on both ends. Land was allocated at Preston to enlarge the joint station. The London and North Western, with the consent of the Lancashire and Yorkshire Railway, was authorised to close the tramroad between Preston and Bamber Bridge and dispose of its site. Tram wagons had ceased to run in 1859 and for several years before that the line had been virtually disused; in 1868 the chimney and engine house on Avenham Brow were demolished. The section from Bamber Bridge to Walton Summit was retained as there was still sufficient traffic to justify it, this was mainly coal for mills. Under a London and North Western Act of 1879 this section too was finally closed, traffic on it having entirely ceased by then.

At the next general meeting following the leasing of the canal, held in February 1865, the proprietors had to decide what should be done about Gregson, the Secretary of the Company. He presented a lengthy statement setting out the history of the canal during his service and his achievements on its behalf and, in conclusion, thanked the committee for their support during that time. It was at first proposed that he should be paid off with £4,500, but this proposal was hastily withdrawn by the chairman. It was then resolved to keep Gregson on at a salary of £1,000 per annum, which was done until his death on December 3rd, 1872. He had given sixty years service to the Company.

The rental now being received from the lease permitted a regular dividend of 1.75% to be paid again and the company invested the £18,293 balance in hand. 1885 saw the final curtain fall on the Lancaster Canal Company when the London and North Western Railway offered to buy the canal outright, to be paid in 4% debenture stock equal to the rental payable under the lease of both ends of the canal. Based on the then prevailing prices this was equivalent to £43-15s-0d for each canal share. The proprietors agreed to the terms and the canal was duly invested in the railway company from July 1st, 1885 under an Act of July 16th the same year. The South End continued to be leased to the Leeds and Liverpool, the rent being paid to the railway. A final dividend of 1.75% was paid after which the Lancaster Canal Company was formally dissolved on January 1st, 1886. A bonus of 10/9d was paid to each proprietor at the last general meeting, leaving a balance of £101-4s-10d which was handed to the chairman. As a memento he had a number of commemorative silver medallions showing the Lune Aqueduct struck. And so ended the Lancaster Canal Company after a life of nearly ninety-five years.

CHAPTER SEVEN:
LATER EVENTS

The winding-up of the Lancaster Canal Company was not the end of life for the canal. Much traffic continued to be carried; in 1824 the committee had sold some land to Kendal Gas Company, thus ensuring regular coal traffic from Preston until the coming of the motor lorry (since there was no access by rail to the gas works). In addition there was coal to be carried to the canal-side mills in Lancaster, and other merchandise such as grain, minerals, manure, timber and chemicals from Glasson to go to Wakefield's gunpowder mills. These mills were by now sited at Gatebeck, further up Crooklands Beck, having replaced the old mills at Sedgwick and Bassingill in 1850. In 1874 the mills were connected by a horse tramway to the canal at Crooklands wharf. However, as the tramway continued beside the main road to Milnthorpe where it connected with the railway, it is probable that the canal only carried a relatively small portion of the traffic during the later years.

The London and North Western Railway managed the canal from Lancaster Castle station where a superintendent was based. In 1883 they opened a branch line from that station to Glasson Dock. Even so, in 1894 the Glasson - Kendal route was still the cheapest for heavy goods such as the cement for Thirlmere waterworks, although by this time the grain trade was dwindling rapidly.

Table 4			
Decrease in Tonnage and Income from the Canal as Shown by the Three Sample Years of 1888, 1890 and 1905			
Year	Tonnage	Tolls	Net Income
1888	173,882	£9,181	£17,289
1889	165,005	£8,013	£18,728
1905	130,396	£6,171	£13,984

The M6 passes by the canal at Tewitfield, which is the head of navigation. Looking up the locks towards Kendal

Apart from a steam ice-breaker, dredger, two Leeds and Liverpool steam tugs and those mentioned in the last chapter, horse haulage was always used on the canal during its commercial life. The steam tugs were tried for a short period after World War I, but owing to the shallow depth of the canal they could not be fully loaded and so were returned to the Leeds and Liverpool. A new craft used on the canal during its later years came and went by sea between Farleton and Glasson.

In 1923 the London and North Western Railway, and therefore the canal also became part of the London, Midland and Scottish Railway (LMS). By an Act of 1935 the LMS received powers to raise tolls and was authorised to close half a mile of the canal at Kendal owing to leakages from its bed, this being done in 1939. Around 1941 or 1942 the canal north of Kendal gasworks was closed. In 1944 the LMS promoted a Bill seeking to close a number of their canals, including the Lancaster. Owing to opposition from several Lancaster firms and from local authorities, all reference to the Lancaster was deleted in the Lords Committee stage. At that time between 6,500 and 7,500 tons of coal a year were being taken by canal to Kendal gasworks since there was no railway access. However, in September 1944 this traffic was transferred to road on the cessation of all commercial traffic north of Lancaster. In 1947 the last goods were carried from Preston to Lancaster, this being a load of coal for Storey's White Cross Mill by Penny Street Bridge at Lancaster.

Upon the nationalisation of the railways in 1948, the British Transport Commission acquired the Lancaster Canal. Under the Transport Act, 1955, they were authorised to close it to navigation and, owing to leakage through limestone fissures in its bed (a problem since Crosley's days), the 5.75 miles north from Stainton Crossing Bridge were drained. The last two miles from Natland into Kendal were filled in. At the Preston end the first three-quarters of a mile has been drained and filled in. The Water Lane Aqueduct has been demolished. A further 100 yards were drained at Holme and pipes inserted, owing to leakage. When the M6 motorway extension was projected, despite strenuous efforts by the Lancaster Canal Trust and other bodies interested in the canal as well as by various individuals, it was decided that there would be five culverts above and one below the locks at Tewitfield, instead of low bridges which would permit the canal's use by pleasure craft. This was done even though the cost of bridges would not have been crippling. In the mid-1970's, on the construction of the Levens Link, the drained canal bed was cut through in two places near Hincaster Tunnel. The reason for the water channel above Tewitfield being retained was because the canal supplied water via a pipeline to the I.C.I. plant at Thornton.

This period was probably the all time low in the history of the Lancaster Canal. Now the pipes at Holme have been removed and replaced by a concrete flume and it has been recommended that nothing further be done to hinder the eventual restoration of the canal north of Tewitfield. 1976 saw a decision by the British Waterways Board (the present owners of the canal to Stainton) to allow powered craft to use the canal above Tewitfield Locks, the first time for nearly twenty years. In the near future, the Ribble Link Trust are hoping that the canal will be linked with the Ribble via Savick Brook at Preston. Much work into the feasibility of this has been done and it is hoped that, with the aid of Lottery cash, the link will be completed around the turn of the century or shortly after. This would give access by boat to the Douglas and the rest of the canal system via the Leeds and Liverpool Canal. Again with Lottery cash, it is hoped that the locks at Tewitfield can be restored, the culverts made into bridges with the top lock being moved back and the canal lowered to pass under the M6, thus opening the way to Kendal once more. First there has to be a detailed study into the £17 million scheme, but it is hoped that work on the actual restoration, which would take up to four years, will commence around 2004.

CHAPTER EIGHT:
THE LUNE AQUEDUCT

The most celebrated architectural feature of the Lancaster Canal is the Lune Aqueduct designed by John Rennie. It is 600 feet in length and 60 feet high, with five 70-foot semi-circular arches supported on rustic pillars with Gothic ends. It is topped by a massive cornice and the parapet is partly balustraded. The aqueduct is the first one for which Rennie used the inverted arch principle, something not visible. Extra strength was provided and exploding arches prevented by building an inverted arch in contact with the other arches where they were most likely to burst outwards with the weight of the cornice. The spandrels, the triangular parts between the arches, hide the inverted arches.

Originally it was estimated that the aqueduct would cost £18,618-16s-0d, an amount subsequently amended to £27,500. Rennie favoured brick for the construction of the aqueduct, but the committee preferred stone. When commenting on the tenders for the masonry, Rennie compared the Lune Aqueduct with brick-built ones on the canals in the Midlands. He wrote to Gregson ".... I still wish the Committee had tried brick, it would have saved many thousand pounds."

The contractors appointed for the superstructure were Alexander Stevens and Son of Edinburgh, while the Lancaster Canal Company undertook the building of the foundations for the piers themselves. In January 1794, Millar, the resident engineer, started the pile-driving within deep coffer dams which had been sunk into the river bed. The dams were pumped dry by steam-pumps, an engine house having been built. In January 1794, William Cartwright was appointed assistant resident engineer and given special responsibility for the foundations.

By July there were one hundred and fifty men working day and night. Troubles arose through drunken engine attendants, the flooding of the coffer dams owing to sudden rises in the level of the river, bad weather and recalcitrant workmen. The piles they made are about 20 feet long, 1 foot wide and 6 inches deep, making a very solid base for the foundations to the piers. The piers from the foundation 20 feet below the level of Skerton Weir, are rectangular to the bed of the river and then have Gothic arches to 2 feet 6 inches above the springs of the aqueduct arches.

By July 1795, in spite of the problems, the piers were complete. They had cost £14,792-9s-8¹/4d (this was after selling off surplus materials and machinery, including the steam engines). Cartwright was presented with a silver cup "as a reward for his extra care in superintending the Foundations of the Lune Aqueduct." The committee also gave themselves a justifiable pat on the back; "Although the cost has been considerable the Committee trust that succeeding ages will give credit and have reason to boast of the permanency of that Work."

Now they were able to proceed with the upper works which went ahead rapidly. The specifications give much detail of the stonework and the way in which the aqueduct was to be built. The arch stones were to be 4 feet long taken in the direction of the radius and not less than 1 foot thick and of no less than 2 feet in breadth. The outside walls between the arches were to be 5 feet in thickness, done in rustic work as high as the cornice, and built in courses not less than 1 foot thick. The wing walls up to the cornice were to be built of the same kind of rustic ashlar (square-cut, dressed stone) as the walls between the arches, and were to have a batter for strength. The mortar for the parts of the work above the water was to be one part of well-burnt unslacked lime and four to five parts of river sand in proper proportions of coarse and fine sand. The puddle for the water channel was to be a yard thick over the whole of the aqueduct. All this detail and more reveals how strongly constructed the aqueduct was to be.

However, Rennie was not satisfied that even this would be sufficient and proposed modifications to give additional strength. Alexander Stevens considered them unnecessary, on which point he received the backing of the committee. Stevens must have had a likeable, friendly nature as well as strong principles because when he died on January 29th, 1796 at the age of sixty-six, both Rennie and Millar wrote movingly of his loss. Rennie was not able to attend the funeral and wrote "I therefore with you sincerely drop a tear to his memory and, had my engagements been fewer than they are," would have been in Lancaster to assist at the funeral." Following his father's death, Stevens' son completed the aqueduct. The last arch was finished in July 1797 and the whole completed in the autumn of the same year, having cost £48,320-18s-10d to build.

On the north-east side of the aqueduct is the inscription "To Public Prosperity," whilst on the south-west side above the central arch is a Latin inscription which can be translated as follows:

"Old needs are served; far distant sites combined;

Rivers by art to bring new wealth are joined.

A.D. 1797. J. Rennie, engineer. A. Stevens and Son, contractors."

There is a memorial stone to Stevens in the south wall of Lancaster Priory Church.

Britton, in *The Beauties of England and Wales,* wrote in 1807 that the aqueduct was considered "the most magnificent structure of this kind that has been erected in Great Britain and may fairly vie with any of the pompous works of the Romans." This still holds good today.

CHAPTER NINE:
THE PACKET-BOATS

It was not long after the Lancaster Canal was opened that the packet-boat service started. August 1798 saw the start of a service on the North End between Preston and Lancaster. In the *Lancaster Gazette* for July 25th, 1801, it was advertised that the packet-boats between Preston and Lancaster "will sail on Sunday morning next at 8 o'clock, and continue to set out every morning at the same hour." In those days, sailing on the canal was considered an adventure. To help overcome this, an advert in 1802 for trips from Lancaster to Preston for the Preston Guild claimed that "for safety, economy and comfort no other mode of conveyance could be so eligible; for there the timid might be at ease and the most delicate mind without fear." May 1st, 1820 saw the packet-boat service extended to Kendal, in competition with the turnpike coaches. The service was advertised to leave Preston at 6.00 a.m., arrive at Lancaster at 1.00 p.m. and the Tewitfield Locks at 4.00 p.m.. Kendal was reached at 8.00 p.m., in time for passengers to catch the stage-coach for the north. The fares for the whole journey were 6/- in the fore cabin and 4/- in the aft cabin. Refreshments, tea and coffee were served on board.

Starting in 1826 there was an additional boat on Mondays to Saturdays, leaving Lancaster at 6.00 a.m. and reaching Preston at noon. It returned at 2.00 p.m. and arrived back in Lancaster at 8.00 p.m. By then the Preston-Kendal boat times had apparently been changed to 7.00 a.m. as an advertisement in the February 25th, 1826 issue of the *Lancaster Gazette* states that they would sail at 7.00 a.m. as usual.

By the 1830's, the threat of the railways was looming, and there was still competition from the stage-coaches. As a result, in 1833 the Swift Boat service was introduced. The first vessel used on this service was *Water Witch,* an iron-hulled vessel built by the Paisley Canal Company. She was 76 feet in length, had a 6 foot beam and could carry one hundred and twenty passengers. A time sheet shows that the service between Preston and Lancaster commenced on April 1st, 1833. The service through to Kendal from Preston sailed on alternate days, the return journey being made the following day. On Mondays, Wednesdays and Fridays the packet left Kendal at 6.00 a.m., arrived in Lancaster at 1.00 p.m. and Preston shortly after 4.00 p.m. On Tuesdays, Thursdays and Saturdays the return journey started from Preston at 9.30 a.m., reached Lancaster at 1.00 p.m. and Kendal at 7.30 p.m.. There were no change in the fares. This swift service was only possible because of there being no locks until Tewitfield. Also, apart from short stretches in Lancaster and Kendal, the towpath was on the same side of the canal for the whole journey. An average of 10 miles per hour to Lancaster was achieved. The boats were horse-drawn, so stables had to be built at eleven horse-changing points. Boathouses were built at Preston, Lancaster and Kendal, and a passenger shed was built at Preston.

On July 22nd, 1833 the Swift Boat service was extended through to Kendal. Apparently, the 57-mile journey was done in seven hours, the horses being changed every four miles. The fares were unchanged and sixteen thousand passengers made journeys in the first six months. Sometimes passengers on the express boats had to disembark at the foot of the locks, walk up, and board a boat waiting at the top (similarly for the journey from Kendal to Lancaster). However, some boats went straight through the locks, with passengers staying on board if they chose to.

The new service proved popular and in March 1834 a second boat, the *Swiftsure*, joined the *Water Witch*. This was an iron-hulled vessel built by Thomas Vernon and Co. of Liverpool. There now began a daily service from Kendal and, in the summer months, a twice-daily service from Lancaster. August 1835 saw a third boat, *Swallow*, join the fleet, but no details of this vessel are known. A fourth boat was ordered in 1839, *Crewdson*, named after the chairman of the Company. In later years this vessel was renamed *Water Witch II* and was eventually used as a canal inspection boat, surviving into the present century.

Crewdson arrived ready for additional services in 1839 when there were two sailings a day each way between Kendal and Preston, with an additional one between Lancaster and Preston. Fares were 3/- in the fore cabin and 2/- in the aft cabin between either Kendal and Lancaster or Lancaster and Preston. Omnibuses ran between the canal and the railway at Preston and timings were arranged so as to connect with trains for Manchester and Liverpool. In addition coaches met the packet-boats at the canal wharf in Preston, taking passengers to and from Chorley and Bolton.

On the opening of the railway to Lancaster, the Lancaster Canal Company halved their fares to 1/6d and 1/-. In wintertime the boats were heated and refreshments continued to be provided on board. Travelling was smooth and comfortable and no passengers were lost to the railway, despite their cut rate fare of 4/- for a combined rail and coach journey to Kendal. *Bradshaw* (the railway timetable) for 1842 includes the connecting times for the packet-boat services between Lancaster and Kendal. The service between Lancaster and Preston was promptly withdrawn, however, when the Company took over the Lancaster and Preston Junction Railway!

From September 1st, 1842, sailings between Lancaster and Kendal left at 7.30 a.m. and noon. The journeys from Kendal left at 8.30 a.m. and 1.30 p.m.. A free omnibus service was provided for the short journey between the packet station and the railway station in Lancaster, where the boats connected with the trains.

A story is told of a near-sighted old lady who wished to make a 15 mile journey to Lancaster so as to arrive in the town as early as possible. Some time after boarding the packet, observing that there was no movement, she asked a member of the crew when the boat was going to start for Lancaster. She was told "Why missis, ye are theer now; come on oot."

Two horses were used on the Swift Boat service; the postilion, usually a boy rode on the second one and drove the first. The boy was obliged to stoop quite low on the horse's neck to pass under the low arches of the bridges. The speed of the boat was regulated by the helmsman, who was known as the 'conductor' or 'master', by giving a blast on a whistle if the boy was going too slowly. If he was going too quickly, a horn was blown. Postilions were changed at Lancaster.

The packet-boat services ceased on September 22nd, 1846, on the opening of the Lancaster and Carlisle Railway's line to Kendal. In 1865, B.P.Gregson wrote that "In 1833 the Swift Passenger Boats were established and worked to profit until the Lancaster and Preston Junction Railway was opened in 1840, and thence maintained a successful opposition to the railway till September 1842......" Gregson himself had been the one largely responsible for the establishment and the success of the Swift Boat service.

CHAPTER TEN:
SNIPPETS

1. Where the canal was cut through a watertight soil, such as clay, no lining was necessary. Everywhere else the canal bed was lined or 'puddled'. Puddling was a mass of earth which had been reduced to a semi-fluid state by working it with a spade, water being mixed in until the mass was rendered uniform. It was so condensed that water could only pass through it very slowly, if at all. A lightish loam mixed with a coarse sand or fine gravel made the best puddling stuff. This mixture was then spread in layers over the excavated channel, the final thickness being anything from 18 inches to 3 feet according to the porosity of the soil. This in turn was covered with an 18 inch layer of soil or poorer clay. Once it had been lined the canal had to be filled with water quickly before it could be damaged by hot weather drying it out.

2. The modern term of 'navvy' derives from the building of the canals when the labourers, often Irishmen, were known as 'navigators'.

3. Rennie's standard bridges, common on the main line from Preston to Tewitfield, are all of the same basic design. The walls curve inwards in plan between buttressed piers at each side of the canal and are battered to give added strength. Below the parapet there is a projecting string course. Although they are called 'standard' it is probable that no two are completely identical.

4. Rennie's 'little aqueducts' are all of the same basic design with modifications as dictated by the problems of the individual sites. The aqueducts have walls which are curved sharply inwards in plan between buttresses at each end. In order to resist the pressure of the water channel they are strongly battered outwards.

5. In several places along the canal, brick beehive-shaped coke ovens were constructed, usually in batteries of three or more. These ovens remained in use until the end of the last century.

The winding hole on the ponded canal at Farleton

6.   There were several accidents on the tramroad bridge, which was situated at the foot of a steep incline. The wagons were attached to an endless chain which was worked by a stationary steam engine at the top of Avenham Inclined Plane. On October 3rd, 1826 the chain broke and the wagons on it at the time ran away, killing two horses under the charge of John Roberts of Walton Summit, an employee of Hall and Company, Canal Traders. Apparently a team belonging to Lord Balcarres, a colliery owner, had landed at the engine when the chain snapped near the engine and fell into the catches of their unhooked wagon, dragging it down the hill. At the time Roberts' foremost wagon (he was moving six in three teams of two horses and two wagons each) was in the middle of the incline. The driver leapt from the wagon and Lord Balcarres' wagon passed by without hurting either him or the horses which were going up the roadside. Roberts' second

72

wagon, which had gone a little way up the hill, passed its two horses, but the wagon from the middle of the hill caught in their gears and dragged them backwards to the bridge. Lord Balcarres' wagon went over them, crashed through the bridge handrail and fell into the River Ribble. One of the horses was killed immediately, the other, in trying to rise, fell over the bridge onto the rocks in the river and was killed. Hall and Company's compensation claim was rejected by the Canal Company as Roberts had infringed a by-law by attaching one of his wagons to the endless chain before the preceding wagon had been detached at the top, the rule being that only one wagon was to be raised or lowered at a time. In 1976 the wagon from the tramroad was found in the mud on the bed of the Ribble having lain there for one hundred and fifty years since this accident.

7. 1976 was one of the few times when there was a serious water shortage in the canal, its level being reduced by nearly a foot. Another major water shortage was one hundred and fifty years before this. On August 25th, 1826 the Lancaster Canal Company's records show that packets could not sail on the North End due to low water levels. Earlier in the month the canal was closed from Tewitfield Locks to Holme, where it was found that the bottom was in bad condition. On August 29th, 1826 traffic on the canal was suspended because of the exceptionally dry weather, a situation aggravated by a burst in Killington Reservoir.

8. It is said that Archibald Millar, who was a surveyor under Rennie, got his levels wrong at Brock. As a result, Rennie designed a tunnel beneath the river. He got Eastburn to check the levels, resulting in the mistake being discovered.

9. In 1974 Bath Mill, which was by the canal at Lancaster, was demolished. During demolition of the tower extension a beer bottle was found cemented into the tower about a yard from the top. Inside was a message written in good copperplate writing on yellowing paper: "This tower was built by four masons and five labourers in the year 1897. Names below: Alfred Grice, Thomas Harrison, Roger Helm, William Thompson, Thomas Eccles, Edward Hock, Thomas Airey, James Dowthwaite, Joseph Hurst, Thomas

Armstrong, drink success to the man who found this bottle." The area where the mill was is now housing.

10.   During World War II water was taken from the canal at Hest Bank to fill the troughs on the railway.

11.   It is on record that in 1889 the drinking water for Glasson was drawn from the canal basin.

12.   Occasionally a stretch of water is coloured with dye when the engineers are checking for leaks (there have been times when the whole bank had given way!) In June 1858, workmen repairing the Roebuck Culvert, 12 miles from Preston, noticed that the water was flowing towards Preston and that the level of the canal had fallen. It was found that the bank had given way at Salwick Moss, 6.5 miles from Preston. Stopgates were put in at Swillbrook, 1.5 miles north, and at Hollinshead Fold, 2 miles south. 60 yards of embankment had given way. Preston mills were cut off from their supplies as a result of the loss of water.

13.   During World War II there was a Canal (Defence) Advisory Committee, but the military left the Lancaster alone.

14.   The paper used for copy letters during World War II reveals economy and paper saving. The backs of old correspondence were used. One letter from the Lancaster dated October 10th, 1941 is on a letter dated July 6th, 1904 from Chaffer and Brundenberg Limited of Manchester to the Chief Mechanical Engineer of the Lancashire & Yorkshire Railway about an enquiry for pressure gauges.

15.   In 1942 there was correspondence on the maximum number of boats which could be operated on the Lancaster Canal. Between Preston and Lancaster it was decided on forty, making return trips, each week. Twenty-four were allowed to use Tewitfield Locks once a week. The same number could use the Glasson flight twice a week. Only the London, Midland and Scottish Railway Company's boats had used the Glasson Arm in the last ten years, so much dredging was needed.

16.   Winter caused problems on the canal and there was wartime correspondence on the subject. The ice was broken by towing the engineer's barge, loaded at the stern so that the bows

The west portal, Hincaster Tunnel, Hincaster, near Kendal

were out of the water. As many horses as possible were used to drag the boat, but it was not very satisfactory as the canal kept refreezing due to heavy frosts. On February 6th, 1945 the ice-breaking boat sank at Garstang, closing the canal for a few hours. Traffic on the canal did not justify an increase in the number of ice-breaking vessels.

17. A work-book for December 1842 shows that employees were working a six-day week. Pay ranged from 2/- to 3/6, the most common amount being 3/2, presumably per day. Jobs were varied covering repairs to locks, work on barrows, painting, quarry work, repairs to railway equipment windows and Thurnham Mill water-wheel.

18. Water was fed into the canal from various sources beside the main Killington feeder. One generous supplier was a Mr Fielding at Calder. According to a letter from Cartwright of July

5th, 1789, Mr Fielding gave the Lancaster Canal Company permission to take water from the Calder and "should always be extremely willing to give the Canal Company as much water as he possibly could, not injuring his own work." He also gave permission for all the water to be taken from the Calder on Fridays.

In 1799 Cartwright suggested that the Keer and the Brock be taken in to provide ample supplies of water for the canal, at about one tenth the cost of repuddling. This was not done.

19.   A syphon, such as the two on the Lancaster Canal, works by taking the stream down beneath the canal and up again to a slightly lower level. The water enters the pool upstream of the canal, drops down beneath the canal bed, then passes into the pool downstream of the canal which is slightly lower than the other pool. This lower pool constantly overflows into the stream bed owing to the pressure of the water coming from upstream.

20.   Most of the bridges throughout the length of the canal are officially named, but local names can be very different. The official names of bridges 122 to 125 in Bolton-le-Sands are Bolton Church Bridge, Bolton Turnpike Bridge, Chorley's Bridge and Bolton Cinder Ovens Bridge. Locally these are often known as Boy's School Bridge, Packet Bridge, Walkden's Bridge (after Granny Walkden who lived in a now demolished cottage by the bridge), and Brow Bridge.

21.   Running by several bridges, particularly in Bolton-le-Sands, are wooden boxes with a higher box in the middle. These carry waterpipes across the canal, the bridge structure being too shallow for the pipes to be buried in the roadways. The central boxes contain a ball valve which prevents any airlocks when the water is flowing.

22.   The canal abounds with wildlife, in the water, beside the banks and in the air above. Apart from many common birds, the kingfisher is also sometimes to be seen darting above the water, as are terns (particularly along the Glasson Dock Arm). Herons may be put to flight, especially along the northern reaches which are ponded. They are elsewhere too; when the author was walking along there preparing this book there was one at bridge number

58, near Garstang. Waterfowl use the canal, particularly mallard and mute swans both of whom favour the more built-up areas where people feed them. There are also moorhens, coots and shelducks to be seen. Various insects, including the dragonfly and damselfly, are around in the summer. Fish caught by anglers include perch, roach, pike and especially freshwater eels. Shoals of sticklebacks are often to be seen and water voles splash into the water as one approaches.

There are many varieties of flowers along the banks such as meadowsweet, yellow flag, water lilies, water mint and many more hedgerow plants. Some areas are particularly lush with plant life, mainly those not walked as often. For the naturalist there is always something of interest to be seen around the canal.

23. On many bridges there are ropemarks to be seen, these occurred when the boats rubbed against the sides of the bridges as a corner was turned. Bridge 98, Lancaster Basin, has an iron plate on the towpath side which is very badly worn by the ropes.

24. In many place along the canal, particularly on the offside, there are London and North Western Railway boundary posts. There is also a stud boundary marker for roadways.

25. From time to time stretches of the canal have to be drained for repair work to be undertaken. In December 1988 part of the canal was drained in Lancaster and an unexploded shell under Penny Street Bridge came into sight. A policeman guarded it until a bomb disposal unit from Liverpool arrived to deal with it.

26. The coming of the canal must have caused a major upheaval in various towns and villages along its line. Nowhere must this have been more so than in Bolton-le-Sands. There the Town End part of the village had its road up to its church cut through. A new road had to be built round the other side of the canal to link the two parts of the village up again. What is now Packet Lane was once part of the main street, but this too was cut and the present road to its left and over the bridge built instead. From Packet Hill, houses on what was the road before the coming of the canal can be seen below. A London and North Western Railway boundary stone is still to be found at the bottom of the hill, just below the post

The sunken horsepath and one of the bridges over the Hincaster Tunnel, Hincaster near Kendal

office.

27. On 13 September, 1997, to commemorate its 200th Anniversary the aqueduct was ceremonially re-opened. A flotilla of boats, led by *Raven* on which were the present Mayor of Lancaster and several costumed characters, including 'John Rennie', drew up at a tape spanning the water channel. Speeches were made, Mrs. Hilda Shuttleworth, the Mayor, cut the tape and then *Raven* led the flotilla over the aqueduct.

28. Finally, if the Lancaster Canal is of interest to you, why not join the Lancaster Canal Trust? The Membership Secretary's name and address is: Mrs Sheila Slater, 91, Cop Lane, Penwortham, Preston PR1 9AH.

INTRODUCTION

The towpath, and the public footpath on the Kendal section are generally in good condition. Footwear suitable for any normal public footpath can be worn. It is only in wet weather, when the path can be very muddy in places, and frosty conditions when it can be slippery, that any problems are likely to be encountered. As it is level, the towpath can be used by virtually anybody able to get outside and walk a little.

Walking the towpath can be done in long or short stages, just as desired. There are many walks along its length which can be done as a round trip involving another path or road or visit to a village. As a rough guide, allow for walking at about 2.5 miles an hour between Preston and Tewitfield and 2 miles an hour above Tewitfield. The slower time for the northern part is because of various diversions round culverts and the number of stiles to cross. These estimates allow plenty of time for looking at the scenery and other things connected with the canal.

Many canal bridges to Tewitfield are numbered and since most are recorded in this guide there is little chance of becoming lost!

Thus overall times for the sections as set out in the book are:

Preston to Garstang	7 to 7.5 hours	17.5 miles
Garstang to Lancaster	5.5 to 6 hours	13 miles
Lancaster to Tewitfield	5 hours	12 miles
Tewitfield to Kendal	7.5 hours	15 miles

A good alternative with shorter walking times that fit in with
b buses and bus routes is:

Preston to Brock	5.5 to 6 hours	13.5 miles
Brock to Galgate	5.5 to 6 hours	13 miles
Glasson to Lancaster or vice versa	3.5 to 4 hours	8 miles
	(Allow about half an hour to look at the dock.)	

Lancaster to Carnforth	3.5 to 4 hours	8 to 8.5 miles
Carnforth to Holme	3.5 to 4 hours	7.5 to 8 miles
Holme to Kendal	6 hours	11to11.5 miles

The Tewitfield Locks

KEY TO MAPS

Canal	━━	Footpath	- - - -
Bridge over	⭢⭠	Railway	┼┼┼
Bridge under	⬕	Cutting	
Lock	⭠	Tunnel	
Road	──	Swing bridge	

**The beginning of the watered section of the canal
from Stainton Crossing Bridge**

Above: **The Lancaster Canal with the hills around the Kent Estuary**

Below: **A pastoral scene near Janson's Bridge, Holme**

CHAPTER ELEVEN:
PRESTON TO GARSTANG

The North End of the Lancaster Canal started originally from behind Corporation Street in Preston, but this part has now virtually all been cleared. To reach the present day terminus go down Corporation Street from opposite Debenhams, across some pedestrian crossings to where Poundstretcher is on the left and Office World is on the right. Continue along the road, past County Library headquarters and to the University of Central Lancashire, which stands on the site of vanished canal basins. Turn left into Maudland Road and cross the railway bridge. From the bridge looking northwards the site of the canal is all filled in, apart from under another railway bridge that carried a line going east. Take the next turning right (Maudland Bank) to Fylde Road and then turn left. At the pedestrian crossing, cross over to Aqueduct Street, cross the road to a small parkland area by the vehicle depot and go through either entrance into the parkland and up to the present terminus of the canal. Looking back towards the station the original line of the canal can partly be determined by some trees, but there are sadly very few signs left of its existence. (Note that there is a bus service from Preston town centre down Fylde Road, should you prefer not to walk.)

Seats have now been placed opposite the canal terminus, looking up the line. A few yards along the towpath there is bridge number 10 (bridges 1 to 8 are on the Glasson Arm) which takes the path over the entrance to the Ashton Basin, the original basin at Preston. From here both sides of the canal are lined with houses, gardens on the offside leading down to the water. Bridge 11 is the first bridge over the canal and has been much widened. Next is Bridge 11a taking Blackpool Road over the canal; formerly an ugly structure, but now replaced with a much more attractive bridge of concrete sections. By Bridge 12 Haslam Park appears on the left, a pleasant spot easily reached from the towpath. Water from the

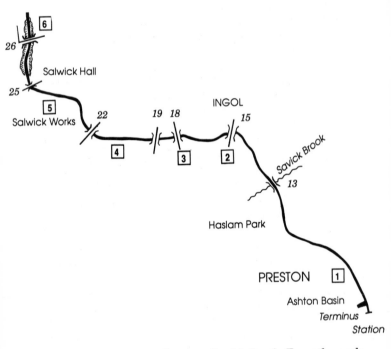

canal is taken off here to flow into Savick Brook. From the park, Bridge 13, the first aqueduct, can be seen taking the canal over Savick Brook. It is here that it is hoped to canalise a route down to the Ribble and then onwards to the Leeds and Liverpool Canal.

Back on the towpath Bridge 14, Hollinghead Fold, is the first of many Rennie 'standard' bridges spanning the canal. Bridge 15, Ingol Ashes, is another but has a pointed parapet rather than a curved one and it is topped with rails. The next bridge, Cottam Mill, is similar but without the rails. From here the canal becomes more rural as the town is left behind. A new bridge, 16A has a winding hole (where boats could be turned) by it and carries the B6241 over the canal. From here onwards the busy railway line to Blackpool is close to the canal which now heads out for the Fylde

82

Plain, coming within 2 miles of Kirkham.

Bridge 17, Cottam Hall, is a skew Rennie standard, not a common type on the Lancaster Canal as most are at 90 degrees to the water channel. Beyond Bridge 19, Harrisons, just before reaching the double pylon line, there was Lea Swing Bridge (Bridge number 20), one of only three swing bridges on the canal. Sadly it fell into bad condition and was removed, so only the masonry on either side of the water channel remains. The bridge served farmland.

Salwick is better known for British Nuclear Fuels Springfields plant than for the canal, only a few fields away. Bridge 25, Wilson's is close to Salwick station which most trains pass straight through on their way to Preston or Blackpool. At various points along the canal, a mile apart, are mile posts which show the distance from Preston on their Preston side and the distance to Garstang on the other.

From Bridge 25 the canal turns north. The moorings here were Salwick Wharf, serving as the nearest point to Kirkham. It was once projected that a canal would serve Kirkham and the Fylde from this stretch of the Lancaster Canal. For the next half mile the canal passes through the attractive tree-lined Salwick Cutting. Bridge 26, Kirkham or Salwick Bridge, is a skew standard which is deeper than normal to accommodate the depth of the cutting. It carries a minor road from Salwick or Kirkham to Woodplumpton or the north of Preston. The canal continues northwards, under the M55 motorway (Bridge 28a) to Bridge 29, Kellet's or Fletcher's Bridge, and then turns eastwards again, away from the Fylde Plain. Here the radio masts of *H.M.S. Inskip* are a dominant feature. Bridge 31, Stone Chimney, is another Rennie standard which has pointed parapets, but is the only such bridge which is skew. Immediately before Bridge 32, Swillbrook, near Catforth is the milestone showing 8 miles from Preston. On the offside of the canal is one of the new signposts now indicating distances along the canal and to the village. Beyond the bridge are the former canal stables and cottages. These have been tastefully converted to housing. Here, is 'Adventure Cruisers' and a slip where boats

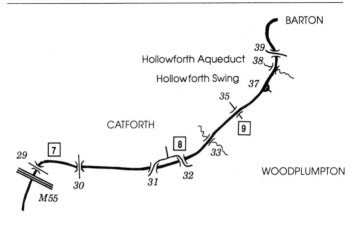

can be launched into the canal.

Beyond Catforth the canal crosses Woodplumpton Brook by a small uninteresting aqueduct, Bridge number 33. By the next bridge, Winneyfield, are stop planks. These are to be found by many bridges along the canal and are for dropping down a slot in the stonework so as to dam the canal at either end of a leak. Bridge 36, Moons, is skew. Woodplumpton village is easily reached from either Bridge 35 or 36. By Moons Bridge is a marina.

Hollowforth Swing Bridge, 37, is one of the only two now left on the canal. It is constructed of wood with two vertical wooden posts on the offside to which are fastened the iron tension rods which support the crossbeams that carry the roadway. The bridge swings on ball-bearings which are on a circular race between the stone foundations. Now it is little used.

A few hundred yards further on is the not very well known Hollowforth Aqueduct, Bridge 38. It is possible to sail or walk over it without noticing. It carries the canal over Barton Brook. A path has been worn for a steep drop down from the end of the aqueduct. A public footpath to Newsham, about half a mile away, passes under the aqueduct which has three arches, the middle one for the mainstream of the brook and the left for the footpath and some

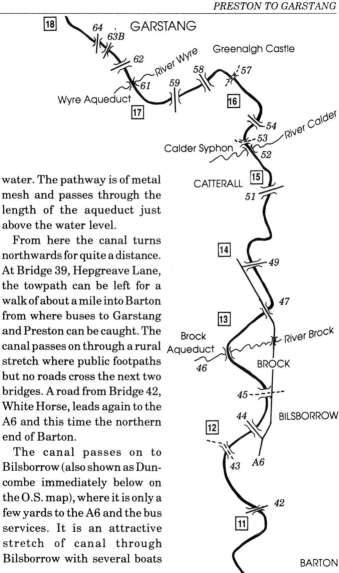

water. The pathway is of metal mesh and passes through the length of the aqueduct just above the water level.

From here the canal turns northwards for quite a distance. At Bridge 39, Hepgreave Lane, the towpath can be left for a walk of about a mile into Barton from where buses to Garstang and Preston can be caught. The canal passes on through a rural stretch where public footpaths but no roads cross the next two bridges. A road from Bridge 42, White Horse, leads again to the A6 and this time the northern end of Barton.

The canal passes on to Bilsborrow (also shown as Duncombe immediately below on the O.S. map), where it is only a few yards to the A6 and the bus services. It is an attractive stretch of canal through Bilsborrow with several boats

85

along the side of the canal; part of the stretch is tree-lined.

Beyond Bilsborrow the canal swings sharply westwards before crossing the Brock by the first of Rennie's 'little aqueducts' (the others being over the Wyre, the Conder and the Keer). To take the river below the level of the canal to a sufficient depth to allow for the strong construction of the aqueduct, it was necessary to dig out to a lower level. Above the aqueduct, which is 23 feet above the river, a weir was built to drop the water to a lower level.

At Brock the canal passes beneath the A6 at Green Man Bridge, number 47, from which it is a short walk to the Preston-Garstang bus stops to the right. Beyond the bridge the canal runs up to the railway line and here is only a few yards from it, the A6 road and the M6 motorway. There are views to the Bowland Fells. The canal continues along a pleasantly wooded stretch to Bridge 51, Stubbins, just before which is a house converted from a stable and attendants' accommodation. Bridge 52, the Calder Aqueduct, takes the River Calder beneath the canal by a syphon. Beyond Bridge 53, Caterall Bridge, is the feeder from the Calder, entering the canal at the basin.

Bridge 54, Ray Lane, lies by the site of the former Garstang and Caterall station, long since demolished. Beyond Bridge 57, Greenalgh Bridge, the ruins of Greenalgh Castle are to be seen. The castle was built in 1490 by the Earl of Derby and was a Royalist stronghold in the Civil War. Now the canal turns south-westwards to Bonds on the outskirts of Garstang, then north-west to Bridge 61, the Wyre Aqueduct. This is the second of Rennie's 'little aqueducts' and has a span of 34 feet. A footpath to Bonds passes beneath. Just beyond lies Garstang basin and then Kepple Lane Bridge, a convenient spot to leave the canal for buses to Preston, Blackpool or Lancaster. Cross the bridge and go straight ahead to the main street.

CHAPTER TWELVE:
GARSTANG TO LANCASTER

Garstang is a pleasant, small market town (Market day Thursday). To reach the canal basin go down Church Street. On the left, just before the bridge, is the entrance to Th'owd Tithebarn, now a restaurant and agricultural museum. The building is over a century older than the canal and stands on the north side of the basin. Unusually for the time, it is built of brick.

From Bridge 62, beside the basin, the canal skirts Garstang. Bridge 63a, Water Pipe, carries a pipe taking water to Blackpool and the Fylde from Barnacre Reservoir. Inscribed with the legend 'FWB 1927', it has a long, narrow arch but does not take pedestrians.

From Garstang to Galgate the canal is never far from the A6 and buses to Lancaster or Garstang. Bridge 63b takes the canal under the A6. This is followed by Bridge 64, Cathouse, from where the canal again takes on a rural aspect all the way to Lancaster. On the offside is Bridge House Marina which has its own separate entrance and exit from the main line of the canal. A few yards further north-west are the remains of the 'Pilling Pig', as the Garstang and Knott End Railway was known. The line has been closed for many years. The bridge was number 65. By it is another marina.

Past Nateby Hall Bridge, 66, the canal turns north-east towards Cabus. Bridge 71, Winmarleigh, lies about a mile east of the hamlet of that name. There are now views to the Bowland Fells to the east and across flat, open country to the west. Along this stretch are several Rennie standard bridges with variations. Bridge 78, Stoney Lane, is railed because during the last war the parapet was taken down to the string course so that any enemy troops would be seen crossing the bridge! Bridge 80, Richmonds, is pointed. There are a number of canalside woodlands along here, making it a most pleasant stretch. The original plantings were to provide timber for work connected with the canal.

At Potters Brook, Bridge 81, the canal is very close to the A6 and,

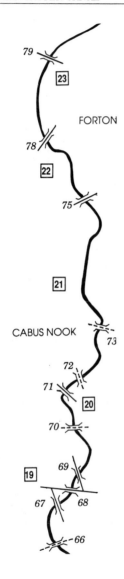

just beyond is the site of Bay Horse Station which was the scene of the rail crash on August 21st, 1848 (See Chapter 5). Bridge 82 is a small aqueduct taking the canal over the River Cocker, a very small river. By Bridge 83, Hay Carr, there are private moorings for the house of the same name nearby. Unusually the moorings are on the towpath side of the canal, not the offside as is normal for private moorings. Beyond here the canal passes through the private estate of Ellel Grange. Bridge 84, Ellel Grange, takes the driveway from the main road and is the only Rennie standard bridge with a pierced parapet with balusters, this being done to suit the setting.

Double Bridge, 85 is a standard of double width. It serves two farms, was built on the boundary and so is divided by a wall down the middle. A few yards beyond this is Bridge number 1, Junction Bridge, taking the towpath over the junction of the Glasson Dock Arm. It is a turnover bridge, so constructed that horses did not need be disconnected from the boats. Whilst of similar appearance to a Rennie standard, it obviously could not have been built until around 1825 when the Glasson Arm was under construction. By the bridge is the lock-keeper's cottage. On the offside, a little further along, there are extensive moorings terminating in Galgate Marina. The village of Galgate is reached by crossing Bridge 86 and turning left. A bus stop is situated here.

Bridge 87 is the third of Rennie's 'little aqueducts' and carries the canal across the River Conder. This aqueduct has buttresses and wing walls on either side and a low segmental

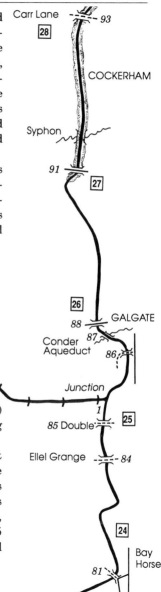

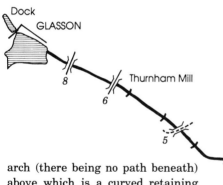

arch (there being no path beneath) above which is a curved retaining wall.

Just over a mile further north at Brantbeck Bridge, number 91, is the start of Deep Cutting. This cutting is roughly 1.5 miles in length and ends just beyond Ashton Lane Bridge, number 94, which carries the A585 from Lancaster. The cutting is lined

89

The Skew Aqueduct, Sedgewick, near Kendal

with trees and most attractive, in the autumn especially. Part of the bed of the canal is cut into solid rock and is not lined. About a quarter of a mile into the cutting is the second of the two syphons on the Lancaster Canal. This one takes Burrow Beck under the canal. It is much easier to see this syphon's way of working than the Calder one's since it is more accessible and the canal is narrower here. In 1794, whilst the canal was being cut through this stretch, the navvies unearthed a major find of the Roman period of occupation. It consisted of seven stone sculptures: two lions, four heads and one of the goddess Ceres. The stones, now housed in the Lancaster City Museum, had apparently been buried in a pit and it seems likely that they came from a family mausoleum of an important Romanised native of the district. Within the cutting is an unusual bridge, number 93, Carr Lane also known as "Broken Back Bridge," probably because the roadway dips to the centre instead of being humpbacked.

As the cutting is left behind, Lancaster Castle can be seen ahead. A short way on, a second path runs parallel to the towpath itself on the same side of the canal. Before reaching Aldcliffe Road the canal passes through another, shallower cutting while the second path passes along the top before dropping down to join the towpath again at the road. The canal turns sharply right at Aldcliffe Road. The following stretch is the only length of the canal where road and towpath are immediately adjacent, with only a fence between them.

Bridge 95, Haverbreaks, is the only standard bridge with no keystone in the arch. Aldcliffe Road Footbridge, number 96, was a ship's gangway that replaced an old pitch pine bridge in May 1954. Originally the gangway was 90 feet in length, but the central 36 feet had to be cut away to fit in across the stone supports. In the road side of the bridge there is a post box; the only one in a bridge on the Lancaster Canal.

The main railway line, formerly the line joining the Lancaster and Carlisle Railway with the Lancaster and Preston Junction Railway, crosses the canal at Bridge 97. On the offside is a two-storey building, just beyond the bridge. It is the recently restored Boat House where the packet-boats were repaired. They were raised by pulleys on the beams of the upper floor. The front of the building is skewed to allow for the launching of these boats. Beyond here is the British Waterways Board yard and there are often work boats about. The yard is reached from Bridge 98, a turnover bridge. Horses could be backed over the bridge without being disconnected from their boats. From here, for a short stretch, the towpath is on the right-hand side of the canal. Beyond the bridge are two large basins surrounded by new housing and then a paved area where the Lancaster Canal Company's offices were sited. Opposite, on the towpath side, is the *Waterwitch*, a public house in the former stables which have been converted and extended. From the basin across from the pub, popular canal tours begin.

The footbridge by the *Waterwitch* was erected for people to cross

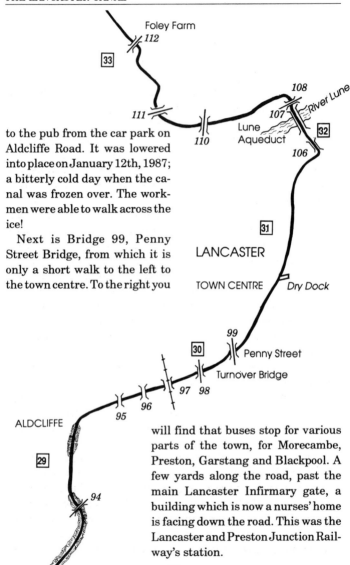

to the pub from the car park on Aldcliffe Road. It was lowered into place on January 12th, 1987; a bitterly cold day when the canal was frozen over. The workmen were able to walk across the ice!

Next is Bridge 99, Penny Street Bridge, from which it is only a short walk to the left to the town centre. To the right you will find that buses stop for various parts of the town, for Morecambe, Preston, Garstang and Blackpool. A few yards along the road, past the main Lancaster Infirmary gate, a building which is now a nurses' home is facing down the road. This was the Lancaster and Preston Junction Railway's station.

92

CHAPTER THIRTEEN:
LANCASTER TO TEWITFIELD

The towpath can be reached from either the Lancaster Infirmary side, or the White Cross side of the road at Penny Street Bridge. White Cross was White Cross Mills, but they are now closed as mills, partly demolished, and the remainder occupied by various businesses and the Adult College. There were several mills alongside the canal in Lancaster, Moor Lane Mills, Bath Mills and Albion Mills, to name but three; all have since been demolished or converted for other uses.

At Friarage, Bridge 100, the canal towpath crosses back again to the left-hand side. The original bridge has been replaced by a modern one and the area around it landscaped. Towering above the canal is St. Peter's, the Roman Catholic cathedral. Bridge 101, Nelson Street, bears the legend 'Joseph Clayton, 1876' and is a widened skew bridge which takes the road to the Trough of Bowland over the canal. Presumably it was Joseph Clayton who widened the bridge. Past Moor Lane Bridge, 102, there are excellent views across the city to Lancaster Castle and Priory Church. Bridge 103, Dry Dock is reached by entering Shaw Street, a street which has old stone flags for the pavement. Just beyond here lies the Dry Dock, the old graving dock, on the offside. The canal passes on through a residential part of Lancaster to a large embankment with a small stream below. Across the canal to the right there is a golf course, along which the canal turns sharply north-west.

It now approaches the Bulk Aqueduct across the A683 to Yorkshire. This modern concrete replacement of a stone aqueduct by Rennie enabled the road to be widened in 1961. For 12 months, while the work went on boats had to be lifted from the water and transported on a cradle and carriage along the gantry on the other side. Nearly 300 boats were transferred in this manner.

Next, the highlight of the canal, the magnificent Lune Aqueduct. This is best seen from below and the river banks can be easily reached from the towpath. Riverside footpaths to Halton and Lancaster pass below the aqueduct and its size and structure is best appreciated from them. The former Skipton to Morecambe railway line passed beneath the southern end of the aqueduct, its line now being one of the paths.

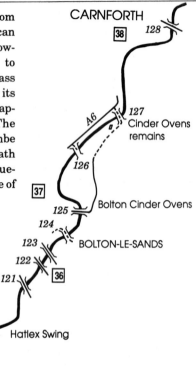

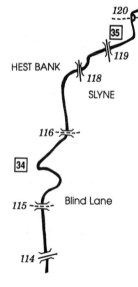

Just before reaching Halton Road Bridge, number 107, there is a small basin on the offside. By it there is an overflow outlet to the Lune and the steady pour of water can be heard. After passing under the bridge the canal turns sharply to the south-west, passing houses on the outskirts of Lancaster. At Beaumont Turnpike, bridge number 110, the canal passes under the A6, the bridge being a much

94

widened standard. Bus stops to Lancaster or Carnforth are close by. After passing Beaumont Hospital on one side and St. John's Hospice on the other, the canal turns north-west to open country again, with views across to Morecambe Bay. Bridge 112 is Folley Bridge, but the farm is now called Foley Farm, one 'l' having been dropped! Belmont Bridge, 114, is sometimes known as Skew Bridge although it is actually the road which is skew, not the bridge. Most bridges are straight across the canal, the roads having been angled. Blind Lane Bridge, 115, is at the end of a narrow lane which led down to stables, most traces of which have now vanished. We are now some 4 miles from Lancaster.

In about half a mile Hest Bank is reached, the closest the canal comes to the sea. The Hest Bank Hotel is handy for buses for Lancaster and Carnforth, while a walk down towards the shore leads also to bus stops for Morecambe and Carnforth. As the canal winds its way from Hest Bank there are good views across Morecambe Bay and towards Warton Crag. Bridge 120, Hatlex Swing Bridge, is the last of the swing bridges, the bridge itself being a comparatively recent replacement.

Bolton-le-Sands is now reached, the canal passing virtually through the centre of the village. There was a Swift Boat service stop here, as is borne out by the name of one of the pubs (Packet Boat Hotel) just by the former wharf. Half a mile beyond, after passing a wood on the right, there is an interesting diversion. One can leave the canal at Bridge 125, Bolton Cinder Ovens, cross over and carry on down a lane to a kissing gate. Pass through this, follow the path down to the canal, through another kissing gate and past the former cinder ovens close to Thwaite End Bridge.This is part of a very old road from Bolton-le-Sands to Carnforth.

On the towpath, from Bridge 125, there are fine views over Morecambe Bay and to Warton Crag and the north. Just into Carnforth there is a large offside marina and also moorings by the former wharf. The canal is only a few yards from the A6 and the bus routes to Morecambe, Lancaster and Kendal. It is only a short distance from here or the next bridge, number 128, into the centre of Carnforth. Trains can be caught from Carnforth station for the

Furness district, Yorkshire, Lancaster and the south. The station featured in the famous film 'Brief Encounter'.

On leaving Carnforth the canal reaches the M6 and a bridge (Brewer's Barn Bridge) leading to exit 35A. Between here and the next bridge the canal had to be slightly diverted to the left to make way for part of the motorway exit 35. Kellet Lane Bridge, 130, although in the country, is controlled by traffic lights owing to its being straight across the canal and having blind approaches. Again, it is a Rennie standard.

The canal now runs nearly parallel to the railway line from Carnforth to Skipton as far as Capernwray, where there is a very good view of the railway viaduct from the towpath. At Bridge 131, Capernwray, the towpath can be left and one can drop down the lane to an old pack-horse bridge. The former

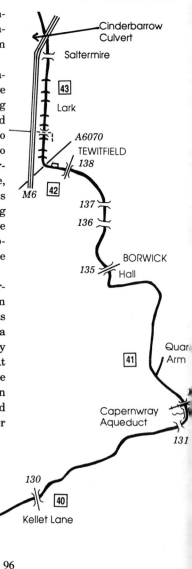

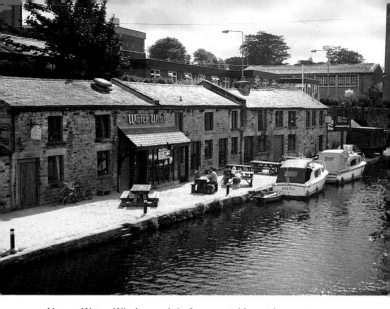

Above: **Water Witch, a pub in former stables at Lancaster**

Below: **The Lune Aqueduct which takes the canal
over the river at Lancaster**

Capernwray Mill, the house nearest the canal, can also be seen adjacent to the last of Rennie's 'little aqueducts' which takes the canal across the River Keer. This aqueduct is quite narrow as the river passes under the canal at the bottom of a steep-sided valley.

From Bridge 131 there is a path on the offside which leads past the caravan site and the remains of loading cranes to a short arm of the canal to Webber Quarry, a former limestone quarry. A public footpath continues beyond here to near Borwick.

Leaving Bridge 131 on the towpath, after passing over the aqueduct the canal goes under the railway and then turns north for Borwick. At Bridge 135, Borwick Hall, the canal can be left for a look at this attractive little village. Borwick Hall, which is easily seen from the towpath before reaching the bridge, is Elizabethan and had a peel tower around which it was built. There are days when it is open to the public in the summer.

From Borwick Hall Bridge the canal quickly passes beneath two more standard bridges, Saunders 136 and Taylors, 137, before bending sharp left for Tewitfield Turnpike, number 138. A short distance beyond lies Tewitfield basin and the terminus of the main cruising section of the canal. Sadly, a good example of a skew bridge was removed here and the canal culverted under the A6070. There is an hourly bus service between Lancaster and Kendal, some of the buses going via Borwick village and the others via Tewitfield. All of them pass through Burton and Holme beyond.

**The Lancaster Canal
near Farleton**

CHAPTER FOURTEEN:
TEWITFIELD TO KENDAL

Across the A6070 at Tewitfield lie the remains of the flight of eight locks which raised the canal 76 feet in three-quarters of a mile. A good view of them can be had from the road above. For several years after closure the locks remained complete, the gates and sluices being left open. However, the large wooden gates have now been removed and the locks weired. The tail bridges have been removed and small service bridges put across the top and bottom locks. The masonry of the locks is still in good condition, one hundred and eighty years after they were built, and they could be restored, although the making of new gates could be expensive. Lock 4 and the adjacent Lark Bridge were restored by volunteers in 1992. So as to take small sea-going vessels en route from Glasson to Kendal, the locks were built as wide locks with two gates. Nowadays the M6 runs by, parallel with the flight until the canal turns to the left just beyond Saltermire Bridge beyond the top lock. It is now necessary to leave the towpath and walk up the road for a few yards before rejoining the canal at Cinderbarrow, the first culvert under the M6 and the point to where the top lock must be removed if the canal is to be restored through to Kendal.

From Cinderbarrow the canal approaches the railway and runs above it (in one part well above) for over half a mile. It then leaves the main line and turns towards Burton. The old Burton wharf is on the offside, just by an aqueduct taking the canal over the road to the former Burton and Holme station. The aqueduct is not visible from above, only from the road. It has a shallow archway over sides which slope slightly outwards from road level. The canal itself still has water in the channel, but to a lesser depth as it is ponded to Stainton, nearly 7 miles beyond. From Burton the towpath is a public right of way (which it is not up to here) through to Kendal.

Nearer Holme there is another aqueduct with a more curved arch, the road beneath joining the road from Burton. The canal

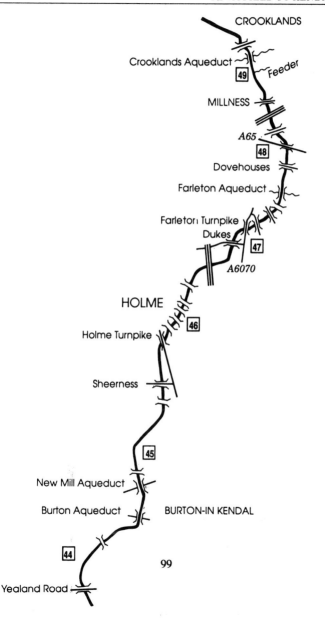

CROOKLANDS

Crooklands Aqueduct

Feeder

49

MILLNESS

A65

48

Dovehouses

Farleton Aqueduct

Farleton Turnpike

Dukes

47

A6070

HOLME

46

Holme Turnpike

Sheerness

45

New Mill Aqueduct

Burton Aqueduct   BURTON-IN KENDAL

44

99

Yealand Road

then passes Holme Mills, a factory colony complete with mill pond and workers' houses. A flour mill had been established here by 1790, before the canal was built. Holme Mills were perhaps the earliest mills in rural Westmorland to use steam power (*circa* 1818). They were rebuilt around 1860, after a fire. The mill chimney has now been demolished.

Half a mile to the north is the village of Holme. Holme Turnpike Bridge (from Tewitfield the bridges do not have numbered discs) is a skew bridge. It seems probable that the Westmorland bridges were an adaptation by Fletcher of Rennie's standard bridge designs, there being a great similarity. This bridge or the previous one are both convenient places to leave the canal for buses for Lancaster or Kendal. Just beyond Holme Turnpike Bridge is a concrete flume replacing the pipes, mentioned earlier, which had been installed in case of leakages in the canal bed. The canal around Holme is popular with canoeists and there are more bridges there than anywhere else on the canal - eight in a mile (the last now being a culvert).

Dominating the canal at this point is Farleton Fell, a limestone crag which has been extensively quarried. Shortly after leaving Holme the canal is once again culverted. The walker has to leave the towpath, pass along the edge of the field by the motorway (Care! There may be an electric fence), then come out by the bridge carrying the Farleton to Milnthorpe road over the M6 which is then crossed to Duke's Bridge. The residence opposite is a former coaching inn dating back to 1630, and after which the bridge is named. The bridge is unusual in that there is an archway in the offside to allow livestock to pass through. To the right, the towpath goes back to the culvert.

After passing under the bridge a disused stable and packet house is reached. Opposite is the Farleton winding hole where boats were turned. Four more bridges are passed in quick succession. Shortly after leaving Farleton there is an outlet to Lupton Beck on the towpath side. Just beyond here is a minor feeder from Lupton Beck which brings water down from Wyndhammere, an artificial tarn near Mansergh. A few hundred yards further on, past Dovehouse's Bridge the A675 crosses the canal on an embankment, the canal being culverted. The towpath passes beneath the road bridge which, if it had been made a little wider, could have taken a water channel, making it accessible to cruising boats.

In another half mile the next culvert is reached at Millness near to Crooklands, where it is necessary to leave the canal, walk under the M6 and rejoin the towpath on the other side. Beyond the next bridge, Millness, the canal reaches Crooklands where there is the main feeder, the water being brought down from Killington Reservoir via Peasey Beck (also known as Crooklands Beck). The beck passes beneath the canal a few yards up from the feeder. By leaving the towpath and following the road back for a few yards, the Crooklands aqueduct can be seen.

Coke manufacture used to be carried out at Crooklands. By 1819 Earl Balcarres, a Wigan coal-owner and one of the canal's proprietors, had a long wharf and several coke ovens there. Today there is still a coal merchant's yard at the wharf, but coal is no longer carried by the canal. The former stables, by the towpath, have been restored by the Lancaster Canal Trust and a picnic area created. The Trust's cruise boat, *Waterwitch*, is moored opposite. She takes passengers for trips along the canal on Sundays in summer.

From Crooklands the canal turns westwards, past a long line of conifers, and then northwards again at Mattinson's Bridge, the second one after leaving Crooklands. Beyond here, on the offside, is the '7 miles from Kendal' milestone. At Field End Bridge the canal turns north-west and, a little further on, west. Here is Stainton Beck, another minor feeder, the water being brought down Saint Sunday's Beck (the name changes at Stainton). Further downstream this beck becomes the River Bela into which Crooklands Beck also flows. Stainton Beck passes beneath the canal which is carried on a small skew aqueduct. A few yards further on, beneath the next bridge, the end of the watered section is reached, the canal being dammed with an earthen embankment. Beyond, other than for the occasional puddle, the bed of the canal is empty and mainly overgrown. Up to this point the canal

101

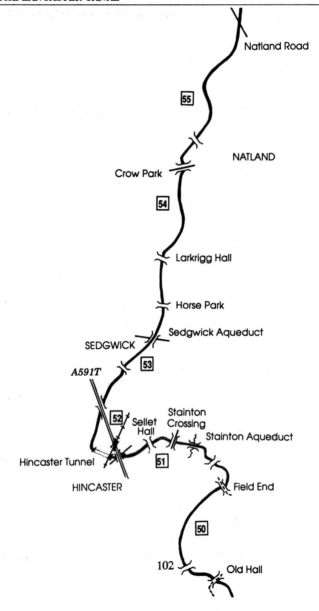

is the responsibility of the British Waterways Board, beyond it is the responsibility of Cumbria County Council. Half a mile further on the canal is again cut by the A590 and is reached again by passing under the bridge, then over a stile on the other side. Ahead lies Hincaster Tunnel, the portals were often largely obscured by extensive growth. The canal bed in front is soft and muddy but is spanned by a viewing platform.

Hincaster Tunnel, 378 yards long, was a place to which boys from Heversham School went for sport. Charles Chandler, who was a pupil there between 1872 and 1879, wrote of those days:

"We fished in the Moss Side brick pond and the canal and caught sand dabs in the bay.

"The canal swarmed with perch and we caught pike by trolling with an "otter".

"All the fish we brought home, Rebecca, the cook fried for us. She was a wonderful woman and cooked eggs, mushrooms, and anything else edible we entrusted to her and every boy always got or thought he got, his own particular egg, perch or eel. We bought apples from the farms and I remember that in 1872 we got 20 to 30 apples for a penny.

"The canal gave us other sport beside fishing. There were always some adventurous boys who were going to swim through the tunnel. I went once with such a party. A bargeman told us the water in the middle of the tunnel was as cold as ice. He said he had boys of his own and would not like to see one of us drowned. I was never a good swimmer, so on this occasion I kept the clothes of those who swam, and by shouts and yells I encouraged them to persevere in their enterprise. But they all came back to my end of the tunnel chilled and subdued, and their limbs felt like cold putty."

There is no towpath through Hincaster Tunnel and the barges had to be 'legged' through or pulled by hand by means of a fixed rope attached to the side of the tunnel. The horses were taken over the hill by way of a separate horsepath, which is still used by walkers. It starts near the eastern portal of the tunnel, climbs the hill, passes beneath the main London-Glasgow railway line and two small footbridges and drops down to the Sedgwick-Hincaster road where the towpath is again joined by the western portal of the tunnel. It is a unique path as it is not part of any road and with its accompanying stonework is a Grade II listed building. The path is in railway ownership and is not British Waterways Board property.

From Hincaster, Lythe Valley damsons used to be transported to their destinations in the south.

The canal runs by the Hincaster road for nearly half a mile until it is cut by the A590, this time more so than anywhere else. It is necessary to walk along the road, past the entrance to Levens Park, over the A590 to a 'Public Footpath' sign to Crow Park Bridge. Go up the slope until a canal bridge can be seen to the left and aim for it. Coming the other way, carry on close to the fence, roughly following the old canal bed, until the ground to the right drops away to a 'V'. The stile is at the bottom of the 'V'.

About three-quarters of a mile to the north-east lies the small, attractive village of Sedgwick. The canal crosses the main street through the village by means of a skew aqueduct, easily reached from the road. The aqueduct is strongly built of stone, very well buttressed and has a stone-lined water channel. The road arch is fairly narrow with the side walls sloping outwards and the top gently curved.

The canal bed remains for a short distance beyond the aqueduct, parts having been made into gardens. Although it is private land there is still a public right of way along this stretch. A stile is crossed into a field and there is a good view towards Kendal from here. The path crosses the landscaped farmland to Horse Park Bridge, now isolated in the middle of the field. Pass under it and go on to a kissing gate by the woodland at Larkrigg Spring. The channel continues for a further stretch through the woodland, after which it is all filled in and largely landscaped.

After passing under the bridge the towpath is fenced off and follows the line of the hedge and crosses fields with views to the outskirts of Kendal. In places cuttings remain to show where the water channel lay (particularly near Helme Lodge). The towpath

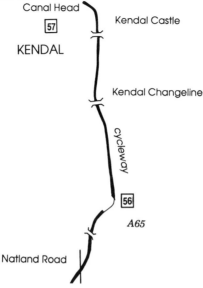

comes out to the Natland road, which is crossed. A little further down a line of trees shows where the canal lay. A sign indicates the footpath to Canal Head, a mile away. From here gardens, car parks and factory yards line the canal bed, but the towpath continues although part of it is now a cycle way. There is no bridge as the A65 is crossed. Ahead lies Kendal Change or Changeline Bridge. Here the towpath crossed to the other side of the water channel for the last half mile to Canal Head. The bridge is now a listed building, and is the only turnover bridge in Cumbria.

Beyond Changeline Bridge were the gasworks which helped to keep the canal open in the 1940's. The last few hundred yards to the canal terminus is a sad ending. The dramatic finish with Kendal Castle looking down on the canal does not materialize and the terminus itself is built over, although several of the buildings at Canal Head North and Canal Head South are those erected originally by Kendal Corporation. By turning right, crossing a footbridge over the Kent and turning left to the end of Blackhall

Road, buses going south can be reached. Alternatively, turn left, cross Miller Bridge and head up into the town centre of Kendal.

The line of trees marks the offside of the canal near Natland Road, Kendal, the filled-in water channel in the foreground

APPENDIX
THE GLASSON ARM

The Glasson Dock Arm of the canal runs from Lodge Hill, near Galgate, to Glasson Dock. It is 2 miles 5 furlongs in length and has a flight of six locks plus the sea-lock. Boats up to 72 feet in length and 14 feet 6 inches in width can be taken through the arm. The total fall between Galgate and the dock is 58 feet 3 inches.

At the junction with the main line (see Chapter Twelve, map p.24) is the lock-keeper's cottage and a turnover bridge crossing the arm. Junction Bridge is Bridge 1. Immediately below the bridge is the first lock in the flight. All six locks are of the same construction and each holds 75,000 gallons of water. The locks are operated by a gate-paddle mechanism which consists of a toothed rack fixed on the side of, and parallel with, the balance arm on the gates which engages with a pinion at the ground end. The mechanism is operated by turning a handle. At the lock end the rack is fixed by a bracket to the top of the paddle arm which moves to and fro in a slot on the side of the balance arm. In operation, as the pinion is turned the rack moves towards either the ground end or the lock end, bringing the paddle arm over and thereby opening the sluice or closing it. The paddles move from side to side instead of vertically, as is more usual. Water enters the locks by means of sluices set into the masonry. Each lock has a side weir to take off surplus water and a tail footbridge for access to the offside. The arm is fed from the main line and the River Conder which flows close to the canal. A channel leads from the river and into the canal at the upper end of Bridge 3.

Above the fifth lock there was a channel leading off from the canal down to Thurnham Mill. The mechanism for controlling the flow of water has now virtually vanished as the channel has been filled in. Until 1976 it was largely intact and in good condition. Thurnham Mill, rebuilt in 1829-30, stands by the sixth lock, the last of the flight. It was originally driven by water power, later by turbines and finally by electricity. Now the building is principally

Thurnham Mill Hotel. It has a three-storey stone-built main block with an adjoining kiln on the north-west end. When it was water-powered, water entered the mill on the south-eastern side where some of the control mechanism still remains today, and was returned to the canal by a tail race below the bottom lock.

The Lancaster Canal Company purchased the mill for £1,100 in 1824 in order to get the water rights and divert the millstream into the canal.

Below Thurnham Mill is Bridge 6, Thurnham Bridge, which takes the Lancaster-Cockerham road over the canal. The Glasson Arm bridges are of a different design from the others, which suggest that they were William Crosley's own work. From Bridge 6 the canal continues in a straight line to the basin. Bridge 8 is a good example of a skew bridge and is the only one of this type on the arm. Glasson's church, Christ Church Glasson, was not built until 1840, fourteen years after the canal, and lies beside the towpath a few yards from the bridge.

Sea-going vessels with tall masts come up the canal to this point but cannot proceed further owing to the bridges. Many such vessels pass through the sea-lock and into the canal basin, which is several times larger than the dock itself. The canal basin is 14 feet deep and covers 36,000 square yards. Here the Lancaster Canal Company had a five-storey stone warehouse (now demolished) which was capable of handling 1,500 tons of goods at once. The former London and North Western Railway branch line from Lancaster (built in 1883) used to have sidings up to the canal. The station was 300 yards away beside the river. Now the line has been made into a linear park for much of its length to Lancaster and is a pleasant walk.

In the corner of the basin at the end of the towpath is the Ba Ba Gee Café, a floating restaurant. On the western side of the basin is a caged weir with a sluice gates to take overflow water from the basin into the dock itself.

The sea-lock can take vessels up to 98 feet in length and 26 feet beam. It is at this lock that the canal ends and the Lancaster Port Commissioners take over all responsibility. The upper pair of gates of the sea-lock are double, one pair facing to the dock and the other to the basin. This is part of an ingenious system to prevent very high tides flowing into the canal basin, the appropriate pair of gates being used depending on which is the higher, the sea in the dock or the canal. Watch is kept on tides of 10.1 metres and above, those of 10.3 metres being level with the canal. The sea-lock is operated by vertical sluices built into the gates, not by a paddle mechanism as in the flight. The gates are opened and closed by chains built into the masonry and are controlled by winding handles on the banks. A swing bridge takes the road between the two parts of Glasson over the lock. This bridge has been con-structed so that its appearance is very similar to the original one, but it is electrically operated and the capstan no longer used. The lock gates and sluices are still manually operated. There are now over a thousand vessels passing through the sea-lock in a year, compared with around two hundred ships in the canal's heyday!

After leaving the canal it is well worth taking time to walk around Glasson and the dock. There is usually plenty of activity. Buses to and from Lancaster can be caught here, but they are very infrequent so a check for timings should be made first if one is not using a car.

SELECTED BIBLIOGRAPHY

Acts of Parliament (various)

The Industrial Archaeology of Lancashire - Owen Ashmore

Baines's *Lancashire*

John Rennie 1761-1821 - T.G. Boucher

The Beauties of England and Wales - Britton

An Account re the building of the Lune Aqueduct. 6th May, 1793 to 1st July, 1795 - William Cartwright

The Lancaster Canal - J.F. Curwen

The Industrial Archaeology of the Lakes Counties - M. Davies-Shiel and J.D. Marshall

The Lancaster and Preston Junction Railway - M.D. Greville and G.O. Holt

The Canals of North West England - Charles Hadfield and Gordon Biddle

A Historiette of the Lancaster Canal - anon. (R.C. Harker?)

Heversham - R.D. Humber

Specification of the Aqueduct over the Lune near Lancaster - with notes by W. Johnson

Lancaster Gazette (various issues)

Lancaster Guardian (various issues)

The Annals of Kendal - C. Nicholson

Nicholson's *Guide to the Waterways (North-west)*

Building the Lancaster Canal - Robert Philpotts

Outlines of an Economic History of Lancaster - M.M. Schofield

Waterwitch (various issues)

Canal Head, Kendal - Paul N. Wilson

In Opposition to the Lancaster and Preston Railway Bill (document)

Correspondence at the Lancashire Records Office

Ordnance Survey maps (various editions) and other maps

Reports to General Meetings (various years)

111